CURIOUS CASES

AND

AMUSING ACTIONS AT LAW

INCLUDING

*SOME TRIALS OF WITCHES IN THE
SEVENTEENTH CENTURY*

THE LAWBOOK EXCHANGE, LTD.
Clark, New Jersey

ISBN-13: 978-1-58477-012-1 (hardcover)
ISBN-13: 978-1-61619-057-6 (paperback)

Lawbook Exchange edition 2000, 2010

The quality of this reprint is equivalent to the quality of the original work.

THE LAWBOOK EXCHANGE, LTD.

33 Terminal Avenue
Clark, New Jersey 07066-1321

*Please see our website for a selection of our other publications
and fine facsimile reprints of classic works of legal history:*
www.lawbookexchange.com

Library of Congress Cataloging-in-Publication Data

Curious cases and amusing actions at law : including some trials of
witches in the seventeenth century.
      p. cm.
Originally published : Toronto, Canada : Carswell Co., 1916.
ISBN 1-58477-012-0 (cloth : alk. paper)
 1. Law--Great Britain--Humor. 2. Trials (Witchcraft)--
Massachusetts.

K184.2. C87 2000
349.42'02'07-- dc21   99-032361

Printed in the United States of America on acid-free paper

CURIOUS CASES

AND

AMUSING ACTIONS AT LAW

INCLUDING

SOME TRIALS OF WITCHES IN THE
SEVENTEENTH CENTURY

TORONTO, CANADA:
THE CARSWELL CO., LIMITED
19 DUNCAN STREET

LONDON:
SWEET AND MAXWELL, LTD.
3 CHANCERY LANE

SYDNEY, N.S.W.:
LAW BOOK CO. OF AUSTRALASIA, LTD.
ELIZABETH STREET

1916.

PRINTED BY
THE EASTERN PRESS, LIMITED,
LONDON AND READING

PREFACE

This is not a law book. The cases and trials are of no legal value to the practitioner. They have been selected solely for their human interest. Lawyer and layman will be entertained alike by the cases in the Birmingham Court of Requests, and will read with pity for the victims and astonishment at human credulity the trials of the witches in the second part of the book.

CONTENTS

PART I.

CASES IN THE BIRMINGHAM COURT OF REQUESTS

Part II.

WITCH TRIALS

PART III.

AMUSING ACTIONS AT LAW.

PART I.

CASES IN THE BIRMINGHAM COURT OF REQUESTS.

INTRODUCTION.

THE cases in this part are taken from Hutton's collection of cases in the Birmingham Court of Requests, the most entertaining law book—if it can be called a law book—with which we are acquainted. It contains ninety-nine cases, of which forty-four are reprinted here.

The Court, of which Mr. Hutton was one of the Commissioners, was established in 1752. He describes it as "the only Court in the English Constitution conducted without a lawyer." It appears to have been needed, as the causes numbered about one hundred and thirty a week. It dealt with causes under forty shillings. Mr. Hutton says:

The creditor is often obliged to reduce his debt to the compass of the Court, which shews his attachment to it. I have known a landlord claim £1 19s. 11d. of a tenant who owed him twelve guineas for the rent of a farm he had left, while he knew the tenant was able to pay the whole; but as he knew him to be a rascal he durst not pursue him in another Court. Here the plaintiff had his choice either to take three shillings

1

in the pound, or throw the debtor into prison for two terms, lose the whole debt, all the expense, and his own place. The debtor too gets quit at an easy rate, either by paying two pounds for twelve, or by lying in prison six weeks, instead of half a year. This is an obvious benefit to trade; the plaintiff has the forty shillings to bring into business, and the defendant four months to labour for himself.

All services must be performed within the pale of the Court. If a man resides in Bordesley, and works in Birmingham, he may be served where he works, but that service must be personal, because it is not his abode; but if he is master of the shop, that reason ceases; it is considered as his home. A person complained " he was served *out* of the manor, consequently the service was null." The Court replied, if he had sent that information by another, they must have quashed the order, but by personally bringing it, he cured the defect; they, therefore, in the laugh of the crowd, entered an order against him. In a case like this, the only danger is to the body; the goods are out of the power of an execution.

After an able-bodied race, between a defendant and a beadle, the former got on the south side of the post which divides Deritend from Bordesley, and the other on the north, and though within a few inches of each other, like Pyramus and Thisbe, they could neither part, nor unite. The defendant defied, and laughed at the poor beadle, while he cursed the enchanted spell, which confined him in the magic circle.

THE PROCESS.

A SUMMONS is first served upon the defendant,
by the beadle of the Court, at the expense of fivepence,
in the name of the clerks, to answer the complaint
of the plaintiff, at a future time, mentioned in the
summons. The Court being assembled, the parties
are called by the crier. If they appear, the plaintiff
is asked, "What is his demand?" If the defendant
acquiesces in that demand, he is charged with a payment equal to his ability. This is the shortest and
most simple cause that can come before the Court, and
is as easily determined without a capacity as with one.
The trial may last half a minute; but if a dispute arises
between two contentious people, it may continue half
an hour, and may require more brains to decide, than
the whole bench can muster. The expense, in either
case, is the same. I have known one of these intricate
causes linger two hours! What other Court would
submit to unravel a crooked cause, during so long a
space, for sixpence?

If the defendant does not appear, the plaintiff pays
fifteen pence, which is charged to the other, and the
cause is kept open for another hearing, that no person
may be taken by surprise. In the interim, an order
is sent to the defendant, specifying the sum he is
charged with, and the manner of payment; to which,
if he has no objection, he need not appear the next
court day, when the cause becomes final. This is the
next class of short causes, and are the most numerous,
requiring no more brains to determine than the other.

But if the defendant supposes himself injured,
he may have a second, or *ex parte* hearing, for six-

pence more; or if either party chooses to postpone
the trial to a future day, for evidence, it may be done
for the same money. Some of these causes are too
difficult for any head to determine.

If any person insults a Commissioner upon the
Bench, the Court can instantly commit him, and carry
him before a Justice, who can charge him with a
discretionary fine under forty shillings. I have known
one instance, in a pert little Jew; we easily reduced
his body, but were unable to conquer that diminutive,
but unruly member, the tongue.

The parties in contest may bring what evidences
they please, but the Court has no powers of compulsion. They are seldom examined upon oath,
because an oath is too sacred to be sported with, though
it may be had upon easy terms; for if a man asserts
a point in open Court, he never refuses to swear it,
neither does it throw light upon the subject. They
have a right also to employ counsel, though I have
never known an instance; pride on one side, and
expense on the other, exclude the black robe. The
attorneys frequently display their oratorical powers,
which are vastly superior to those they display upon
parchment; perhaps attention is paid to language
which many *hear*, but none to writing, which no one
reads. One short remark characterises the keen-eyed
fraternity; they always endeavour to throw us off
the basis of equity, and goad us with points of
law.

NONSUITS.

FROM the ignorance, or forgetfulness of the suitors, many errors are committed, which are always attended with some expense. If a beadle serves the summons, and the plaintiff should not appear to prosecute his claim, a nonsuit ensues. If a plaintiff neglects to attest the service, the cause having lost its support, drops into a dismission; but if he neglects to prove the service of the order, though the Court ought to dismiss the cause, yet out of kindness they will continue it two or three Court days, at 6d. each, to give him a chance of amending the error. But if the defendant should appear on any of these days, it becomes a nonsuit. I have known a plaintiff nonsuited even in Court, by not attending to his name when called. I have known a defendant inveigle the plaintiff down stairs, to whisper a secret, while he knew the cause would come on, and as the service could be proved by the beadles, he has non-suited the enemy. I have known one man nonsuited by leaving the Court, only to take in a pint of ale, and another to let one out. As a list of causes hangs up for inspection, in open Court, a man will retreat for an hour or two, supposing, by the number of his cause, it may come on at such a time. Business may go off quicker than expectation, when, at his return, he has found a string of half a dozen nonsuits to pay for; is laughed at by his competitors for victory, quarrels with every person present, and with himself the most.

FEES.

THE fees of office are complained of as burthensome by all, except him who receives them; and the complaint is too often just. Every man ought to be paid for his service, but one man should never have the power to fleece another. Exorbitant fees are a stagnation to business. Whether a Court sells justice, or a mercer a suit, if they sell upon easy terms, they will both acquire custom.

The fees of this Court, which are easier than those of any other Court of Requests within my knowledge, are wholly the property of its officers. The Commissioners have all they ought to have—nothing.

One fee, belonging to this institution, has given me some concern. It ought to be paid, but I cannot fix upon the man who should pay it. Though warranted by the Act, it carries the air of injustice. The moment a person is taken in execution, he is a prisoner to the beadle, and whether these two continue together six minutes, or six weeks, five shillings is paid to the beadle whenever they part. It is cruel to charge this payment upon the plaintiff, for by the other's confinement he has already lost his whole debt, and expense; he would sustain a second injury, instead of finding relief in the first.

It is unjust to charge it upon the prisoner; he has undergone a punishment equal to the fault. As he has suffered all he ought to suffer, no further demand can be made. His imprisonment indicates poverty, and to saddle him with the expense would keep him still a prisoner. Five shillings is a serious thing to him who has none.

Nor can the loss be sustained by the beadle; he cannot run a hazard in taking the defaulter, nor find materials, pay rent, keep servants, and work gratis. However inequitable, when the defendant discharges the debt by imprisonment, this irksome tax is paid by the plaintiff.

A table of all the fees, except the above, which will scarcely bear the light, is hung up in open Court, and are as follows:

For every summons, to the clerks 3*d*.

For the service, to the beadle 2*d*.

For calling plaintiff, or defendant, clerks 2*d*., beadle 1*d*.

Nonsuit, to the clerks 1*s*.

For paying money into Court, to the clerks 6*d*.

For every hearing, to the clerks 3*d*.

For a copy of every *ex parte* order, and of every judgment of nonsuit to be served, to the clerks 4*d*.

For the service of every such order, to the beadle 2*d*.

For every execution, clerks 8*d*.

To the beadle for levying the same, 1*s*.

For acknowledging satisfaction in full, clerks 4*d*.

For every search, to the clerks 2*d*.

When I first sat in this Court the clerks and the beadle were under a private contract; the beadle was chargeable with every expense, was to pay the clerks an annual stipend, and appropriate the residue of the profits to himself. This genius of the Court was William Bridgens Barton, nominated *Gentleman* in all deeds of lease and release; who, though possessed of about ten thousand pounds, was seldom master of a shilling, but frequently borrowed a trifle of his own servants, to pay his reckoning or to satisfy a kind nymph. Notwithstanding this barrenness of cash a stranger would think he was fond of money, for his littleness of temper would at any time suffer him to run of an errand for twopence. He was equally averse to receive and to pay money. If he accidentally met a person in *his* debt, he shunned him by running away, or hiding himself in obscurity. If one came to pay, " Let it be " was the word. Those who dunned him always found him in haste, received ample promises, forgotten in a moment; but his good nature, of which he had a large portion, always warded off the blow. Though he daily gave and took credit, he kept no private books of account; his counting-house was his memory, which was very retentive; but when he died it was locked up with its contents for ever. He was landlord to a farm near twenty years, without ever receiving a shilling rent. Always in a hurry without making progress; he dispatched nothing quick but the tankard. Expedition never discovered itself but in getting drunk, in which he became so expert, by daily practice, that he could accomplish it in ten minutes. I have known him drive a post-chaise to Warwick for as much liquor as he could tun into his vessel. It was indifferent whether he slept in a bed, upon the hearth of an alehouse, or under a manger; or whether he staggered thither, or was carried. He wrote an excellent hand, was master of figures, and well understood the business of an attorney's office. His fondness for employment induced him to work without profit; and yet, from his random conduct, his employer became a loser. His shoes received their last tincture of black from the currier. It was of no consequence to him whether he wore his shirt a week or a month, whether his neckcloth was tied under his chin or his ear, or whether the top or the bottom of his wig was uppermost. His beard and his linen were equal strangers to the suds.

The money belonging to the suitors must of course pass through the hands of this good-natured sloven, or, rather, pass *into* them, for it seldom came out. The result was the Court dwindled, the suitors complained, the Bench remonstrated, *he* promised, the evil grew, and the clerks were obliged to take their department into their own hands; since which time it has been conducted with prudence.

All sides were pleased, and the current of property was now to run in its right channel. Still, by the laws of his office, the money arising from executions must submit to the touch of his fingers, and we were again obstructed. "Of what use is the Court," says the suitor, "if we cannot have justice? We had better lose our money by the debtors than be defrauded, at another expense, by the beadle."

The Commissioners entertained serious thoughts of discharging him, and perhaps three months would have finished their purpose, if, in the interim, the strength and quantity of his liquor had not sent him into another world, where he could not conduct matters much worse than he had done in this.

I.

THE PLEASURES OF MATRIMONY.

Law, with its rigid fetters, binds what conscience sets free. Law knows no mercy. Equity knows no rigour. If this Court cannot proceed contrary to law, they can proceed without it. Nature has furnished every man with the talent of judging between right and wrong; the paths to both are straight and even, though the light is sometimes defective.

It is a duty, an interest, and a pleasure for a man in the conjugal state to promote *his own* happiness. If he lives in amity with his wife, he fully enjoys the benefit himself. There is no species of happiness more interesting, none will better pay for cultivation, none is so much neglected. Love is the foundation of this felicity, and this often rests upon prudence. If love does not exist, happiness cannot. If a man is unable to love his wife, let him try to pity her; none ever repented, or went unrewarded, who made the trial; if she has not his affections she merits his pity, and pity is the sister of love. He will suffer more by hating *her*, than himself. He can easily excuse his own faults; let him try to excuse hers. He who barters happiness for caprice, may improve by reading Paul's sentiments upon this subject to the Ephesians, or, if sacred sounds hurt the ear, he may find an excellent lesson in the old song of Darby and

Joan. On the other hand, if the husband is to love his wife, the wife can do no less than try to deserve it.

George ——— and Ann his wife lived together, like other new married pairs, in great harmony. They lamented they had not entered into marriage and happiness sooner. But alas, the smile, the moon, the dear, and their loves, waned, wore out, and changed together. These were succeeded by the sullen look, the back turned where the face should be when a question was asked, and a cold answer given in the monosyllable " No." The dainty bit was now cut for dear self, which used to be offered to *dearest life*. She exercised her tongue upon him, and he his foot upon her.

Matters cannot always grow worse; they will come to a period. It was prudently judged, if two people must plague each other, they had better plague at a distance. If it was better to marry than to burn, it was better to part than to kill. Our couple, who possessed more wisdom than love, chose, like their superiors, to separate. But here a difficulty arose: How could a maintenance be obtained? George hated economy, and madam hated labour. George thought it cruel to work for one he detested, and she could prove from Scripture, under the very hand of Paul, that a wife ought to be supported by her husband.

Her friends were consulted, and, by an indenture tripartite, George was to allow her twelve pounds a year, and be screened from all demands she should make, or debts she should contract.

If a woman spends twenty-four pounds, she will find it difficult to cover that sum with twelve. This being our case, the result was George was pestered with duns, arrests, and suits in various Courts. All

this did not diminish their love, for they had none.
Among other Courts, George was brought to the Court
of Requests.

After the necessary enquiries into the nature of the
debt, the Court remarked: All our laws, both statute
and common, charge the debts of the wife upon the
husband. Though in her family she may possess
absolute power, that power is usurped, the law gives
her none. The act of the wife is deemed the act of
the husband. It is necessary the husband should be
responsible, or the creditor would have no security
for the property he parts with. But in a case like this,
where terms of separation are agreed on, published
to the world, and known to all who know the parties,
none can plead ignorance. A contract like this ought
in reason to be as binding as that of marriage.
Though the law allows no separation without a divorce,
yet it ought to be accepted, lest worse mischiefs
follow. If we admit this doctrine, the parties may
live comfortable asunder; if not, the husband is
inevitably ruined. He is in the power of a revengeful
wife, who may contract what debts she pleases. She
may draw his whole fortune. A new gown would
clap him into prison, and a milliner's bill make him
fly his country. While the husband fulfils the original
agreement by paying the twelve pounds per annum,
which, by the way, is as much as his circumstances
will allow, we will not make an order against him;
if he fails, we will. Whoever trusts the wife trusts in
her own honour, for her person is secure, which ought
not—but his ought.

II.

THE STURDY CLUB.

PUBLIC faith, and private benefit, are the same thing; they tend to the same point. Two parties make a solemn bargain with each other, and both keep it *while it is their interest*. He who happens to become the first sufferer is dissatisfied, feels the yoke sit uneasy, and exerts every effort to throw it off his shoulders, while the gainer loudly complains of his injustice, not considering that circumstances only differ; the men are the same, and if the tables were turned each would act the part of the other. The criterion of justice is a man's own sentiments, and those sentiments are founded on his own interest.

Two members of a sick club sued the stewards for their weekly pay. The stewards alleged they had nothing to do with the matter, for the club was dissolved. This club had long existed, but being frightened at their two brethren, likely to continue sick for life, had put a period to the society.

Court: By what authority did you dissolve the club?

Stewards: By consent of the majority.

Court: If a majority can dissolve the union, what security is there for a sick member? No covenant can be made without the consent of two parties, neither can it be dissolved without the consent of both. The majority you mention is but one party, a sick man is the other, and the covenant holds firm till dissolved by their joint consent. As you are a body of men united for your common good, you have a code of laws to support the compact; shew us the law that enables you to dissolve the union.

Their articles were produced, among which was one expressly forbidding the dissolution while three members refused their assent. The Court was crowded. The body of the club were assembled to support their imaginary stewards and to hear the result of a trial interesting to all.

As the cause did not seem to turn much in their favour, they insisted upon a continuance to a future day. This the Court will not refuse, provided light can be thrown on the subject, and there appears no views of delay.

Finding themselves the weaker side, they applied to a lusty lawyer of Northfield, who, like Nero, was born to keep the world in awe. He wrote to the Commissioners, in which he drew out all the artillery of the Courts above, pointed it at their devoted heads, and threatened destruction if they proceeded against the club.

The same ground was trodden over the second hearing as the first; when the club, finding the Bench were not subdued by their powerful auxiliary, solicited a third hearing, which was granted; when the man of Gath appeared, formidable at the head of his troop. He contended that no action could lie against the defendants; that they were not stewards; that their time had been long expired; that they could not be sued for the money they never received; that the club did not exist, for the body of men which had formed themselves into a society had a right to dissolve it; that the consequences of an arbitrary decision would be dreadful, and that he was authorised to commence an action.

Court: We must accept the defendants as stewards unless you can make a subsequent set appear. We consider the club to exist, because, as there are three objectors, it has not been legally dissolved. The man who enters into a bond cannot cancel it of himself. A bargain is binding till dissolved by all the parties that made it. We should dread an arbitrary decision more than we should your action. The intent of a club is to support the sick, which is not done by quirk, bully, or finesse, but by a fair distribution of that money which the afflicted have a right to. A box loaded with sickness cannot warrant a dissolution. They are bound by their own laws, and we must lend our aid that those laws may not be broken. The whole is an act of their own, and they must abide by the event. We are sorry to draw money from the stewards, who perhaps have none besides their own, but justice demands it. We can, however, put them in a way to reimburse themselves: apply individually to the members, and if any refuse to pay their share bring them here, and we will enforce payment. We must give judgment for the plaintiffs.

The attorney d——d the club for ignorant fools, who had misinformed him; the club accused the attorney for promising more than he performed, and the stewards went away satisfied.

III.

THE CARRIER.

LET me open for your inspection a common page in the history of a trial. When a cause commences it perhaps gives a shock to the mind, equal to that of electricity to the body. The internal powers rise into a ferment, like ale in a vat. One party, perhaps both, privately brings his summons, perfectly clean, his cause piping hot, and himself out of breath, to a Commissioner.

"Sir,"—wind meeting wind, chokes his words in the gullet, his hat covering the right ear—"Sir, you hold the Court of Conscience."

No, sir, I do not.

"I thought you had sat there!"

I do not sit *here*.

"I only wish to open an affair that will come before you"——

Had not you better keep it shut till it comes, with the parties, before the Bench?

"Only, sir"——

But what will the world say if I try causes at my own house? What will your antagonist say if he knows you have received a private opinion from me?

"He will never know it."

He shall not. To give a sentiment here is an affront to the Bench. You can have no motive for applying to a Commissioner but to prepossess him in your favour, which is taking an unfair advantage of your enemy.

2

" Only hear, sir, he has used me d——d ill "——

Is that a reason why you should use me ill, in forcing your cause upon me, which perhaps is bad, or why are you solicitous that I should mend it? You have differed with another, and if I do not join in your sentiments you stand a fair chance to differ with me.

" I only want to *incense* you in the affair, which is "——

I do not want to be incensed, neither have I *time* to examine cases; I willingly allow a large portion to the Court, but it takes a larger, nay, it is with great difficulty that I can prevent it from taking all. If I appropriate one day in the week to the Church, and another to the Court, I wish to possess the remaining five myself. Necessity obliges me to repel private applications, or every moment of my life would fall a prey to the Court. A public shop, in a central situation, furnishes an easy access for the suitor. I must either speak, or hear others, round the twenty-four hours. Cut off from business, rest, amusement, food, and sleep the animal would sink under the weight. I am called from the private avocations of a family, dragged from the interesting connections of a friend, to decide upon a cause partially told. My ears are doomed to receive the same words ten times repeated, or disoblige, when I wish to avoid it. If I am casting up an account of 500*l.* a stranger, like you, can break in without ceremony, and kick down the fabric in a moment. My rest is interrupted, my meals sported with—nay, I am even called out of bed for an opinion; for where one man *gives* what another wants he will never want custom. Warmed with his own cause, the solicitor forgets I am liable to take cold, while he detains me a prisoner half naked.

" 'Pon my word, that is very wrong!"

You, as keensighted as the rest, can behold the mote in the eye of another, but not the beam in your own. You now offer me the same wrong in a less degree, and, like every applier, only wish me to favour *your* cause, and allow me to reject every other.

Materially interested himself, he cannot yet give up the argument, which obliges me, at last, to finish it with a frown, or a flight.

Disappointed in his expected auxiliary, he tries the cause in his own bosom, musters every argument and every evidence in his favour, and wins his ground with ease; for in every contest, both parties expect to rise victorious. But alas, when the cause opens to the Bench it appears he had only mustered the evidences on his own side, and forgot those on the other. Thus his visionary mansion dissolves in air. Had I attended to his story, he might have deceived *me*; had I given a judgment upon it, I might have deceived *him*. No man can pronounce fairly without hearing both parties. No party ought to be heard except at the Bench.

A manufacturer sent a parcel of goods, value three pounds, to a shopkeeper, at a market town in Leicestershire, and when he delivered it to the carrier ordered him not to part with the goods without money. However, by some little neglect in the carrier, and a little finesse in the shopkeeper, he got possession without payment.

During about three months the manufacturer repeatedly applied to both, but without effect, when the shopkeeper failed. The carrier was brought to the Court. Each of the contending parties made private attempts to win the Commissioners, but, like the priests, who had quitted the confessional chair, they could not attend either to truth or falsehood.

The carrier insisted he had nothing to do in the matter. He was only the hand through which the goods passed. That he did not find out the shop-keeper, sell him anything, nor get anything by him, therefore had no right to be responsible. That the manufacturer did not look upon him as paymaster, or why did he apply to the other?

Court: Had no injunction been laid upon you at the delivery of the goods you had stood clear; but that injunction was part of the bargain, the terms upon which *he* sent the parcel, and *you* carried it. If the shopkeeper did not pay you, you had a right to bring it back, and charge double carriage, but none to leave it. His asking the shopkeeper for payment no way affects the question; you are both responsible for the money. He can claim upon the shopkeeper, you cannot. But if you pay this money, you can claim, and he cannot, except for the one pound and a penny, which we will persuade him to give up in consideration of your carriage and your loss. We must decide against you, or put a period to verbal agreements.

IV.

THE EXECUTOR.

A PERSON died to whom the plaintiff owed six pounds. The executor of the deceased made several applications for payment. The plaintiff gave him a fifteen-pound bill.

Executor: I have no cash to give you in return, and it will cost half a crown to get the bill discounted, which I expect you to pay.

Plaintiff: I will not pay a farthing, but will take the bill again.

Ex.: Leave it with me, and I will try to procure the cash.

When the plaintiff returned for the bill, or the balance, the executor stopped half a crown, which the plaintiff, not consenting to, applied to the Court for redress. The executor, by his attorney, urged in defence, that he considered himself only as an officiate under the will of the deceased; that he had nothing for his trouble; that he had lost much time in soliciting payment; that it would be unjust to oblige him to pay the money out of his own pocket, and that he had made a reasonable charge.

Court: Your accepting the office of an executor was an act of choice; you are, like every other person in the same situation, answerable for the errors you commit. If the plaintiff procrastinated payment, the compulsive power was in your own hands. We shall not enquire into the reasonableness of the sum for discounting the bill, but whether you had a right to do it at all. While it was another's, you could not

bring upon it any expense; while it was yours, you
could not bring any upon the plaintiff. A decision in
your favour would draw after it a train of evils, which
ought not to exist in a commercial country. A
receiver might then, from caprice, discount any bill,
perhaps at a dear market, and the payer, without any
consent of his own, be subjected to an arbitrary
demand. Had he consented to pay the discount, you
had gone upon sure ground. A receiver may return
a bill, as well as a light guinea, and demand something better in payment, but he cannot sell either
without the consent of the owner.

V.

A JUDGE MAY QUIT THE LINE OF JUSTICE.

It is an established opinion that "there is no
general rule without an exception." This maxim
holds good in equity. Every man ought to have his
own, and the Bench ought to assist him in recovering
it. But there are cases, though they rarely occur,
where the Bench ought to act against the injured, and
even assist the culprit. This step is out of the reach
of law, and can only be attained by equity. Law
knows no attribute but that of justice; equity can
introduce mercy. Law gives a man his right; equity
sees cause to deprive him.

A person sued a poor old infirm man. The debt
was just.

Court: It appears from the circumstances before
us that this man is not master of one penny; he never
will be able to earn one. He possesses no property.

There is nothing he can call his own, but age, sickness, and poverty. He is one of those few that a thief cannot plunder. He never will eat, but at the expense of another. It is remarked of age and infirmity that a man has "one foot in the grave," but this miserable object may fairly be said to have two. We wish you to withdraw the action.

Plaintiff: The money is my due, and I will not withdraw it.

Court: His non-payment arises from inability, not from obstinacy; and this inability will never be removed. It is cruel to punish a man for not doing what he is unable. We may as well attempt to strike money out of a flint as out of him who has none. As a few weeks, at the utmost, will finish his wretched existence, and as common humanity forbids us to suffer him to die in prison under our warrant, we shall set the payments as low as the Court can allow, and protract the first for three months, by which time he will, in all likelihood, be removed to that place where stern justice never frowns through the features of a creditor.

VI.

MATCH A KNAVE.

IF you cannot catch a knave in *your* trap, catch him in his own.

The stewards of a sick club sued a member for the arrears of his weekly contribution. He pleaded his nonage.

Court: Are you married?

Defendant: Yes.

C.: And so you are, at the same time, a husband and an infant. Was it honest in you to enter this club, and, if attacked by sickness, to draw money from the box, and yet, to prevent paying what was their due, shelter yourself under childhood?

D.: I have never received anything from the club, consequently I owe nothing to it.

C.: So much the better that you never had *occasion* to demand from the box; but every member, though he enjoys a series of health, receives a constant benefit from it, for the very idea of a support in the day of affliction yields to the mind a daily satisfaction. Health may be better enjoyed when there is a treasure laid up for sickness. Your not receiving is no argument why you should not pay. You continually held a claim in reversion. As we cannot precisely determine a man's age by looking in his face, we have a right to demand a certificate of yours.

The next Court day he produced one from the Church register, by which it appeared that twenty-one years had elapsed within three or four weeks.

Court: This proof does not come up to the point. What age were you when you were baptized?

D.: I cannot tell.

C.: A man arrives at maturity twenty-one years after the day of his birth, not his baptism. We generally suppose a child may be a month older than the date of the register. But in cases where one party wishes to defraud another it becomes necessary to draw the line with precision. If we strictly adhere to a register, it follows, those children who are not baptized till three or four years old will not be of age till four or five and twenty; nay, we have known instances of people being baptized at forty, which

would give them a licence to do, what they often do
without—cheat the world till threescore. As you
cannot ascertain your exact age we shall set aside your
childish plea, and do you the honour of treating you
as a man; an honour you would gladly accept in any
place but this.

VII.

THE SECOND-HAND WIFE.

EVERYTHING is great or small by comparison. As
this is a little Court I can treat the reader with only
little matters. The man who deals in pounds will
view shillings as trifles; but one shilling is a serious
thing with him who has but two. Diminutive as this
Court appears, it often grasps a sum equal to the
whole fortune of a suitor. If then it seems little to
the great, it is really great to the little; and yet, when
I have seen, in a superior Court, a Judge in tremendous
scarlet, nineteen counsellors, who may be deemed
expletives in society, watching, like birds of prey, to
feed on the carcass of contention; a jury with twelve
serious faces, and a crowded Court amply officered,
all attentively employed in a twelvepenny cause, which
I thought was rated at twice its value, I have considered this grand Court, with its superb furniture, as
completely little as that I describe. The higher the
characters who condescend to play at push-pin, the
more ludicrous the act; the greater the number of
people employed about——nothing, the more they
excite risibility.

Though the Commissioners have no right to clothe
themselves in terror, neither do they practise it;

though majestic looks, and a paltry office, are a miserable jumble of things, yet I have observed even the great tremble before them. I have seen the Bench put on a smile, to encourage the diffident, to stop the trembling hand, to assist the faltering tongue, dispel the rising tear, and, if presuming arrogance attempted to bear down an antagonist, they have supported the weaker side. Truth does not always lie with the most voluble speaker.

A huckster sued Risby for goods sold to his wife, at various times, for the maintenance of the family. Risby declared he had nothing to do with the goods, the debt, or the woman; that he never was at the shop, that she herself fetched them, that they were consumed in her own family, that he was only an inmate, and that, instead of her being his wife, she was wife to another man. These powerful assertions were uttered in a tone that seemed to rise superior to the enemy.

Court: Did you partake of the huckster's property?

Risby: If I did, I paid the woman for it.

It appeared from various evidences that she had a husband, who had entered into the army and left the kingdom some years; that Risby and she had long cohabited together, as man and wife, and passed for such in the eye of the world. She had taken his name, and had one child by him.

C.: By evidence, which we have no reason to doubt, you kept but one table and one purse, as well as one bed. You know the goods were bought in your name, and upon your credit; therefore you cannot plead being taken by surprise. If to deny a fault adds to the guilt, it follows an error diminishes

by confession; consequently yours is doubly reduced,
for you tacitly acknowledge two, living in adultery
and cheating your neighbour. Had your designs been
honourable you might at any time have put a period
to the growing account. The goods were entered in
your name, which shews that name was offered as
the responsible one to the huckster, and this could
not be offered by any but the wife you owned and
trusted. As you partook of the purchase it is reasonable you should pay for it. You observed, you paid
the wife; but an assertion, particularly from a faulty
character, is no proof. We can easily believe you
frequently gave her money, or the family could not
have subsisted. But the most material reason why
you should pay is, you passed before the public as
man and wife; you gained credit upon that supposition.
We only take you to be what you offered yourselves
to be. If there is a deception, it was fabricated by
yourself. We cannot examine registers, to find out
who are married, in the cases before us. If a plea
like yours was allowed, but few people could recover
their property; the burden would be shifted from one
to another till nobody could be found to bear it.
During your cohabitation together you are responsible
for her conduct as a wife. We shall make an order
accordingly. If you are aggrieved you have a remedy
in your own hands by charging the real husband with
what you pay for his wife; but perhaps it might seem
rather singular to saddle that husband with an aug-
mentation of debt, and of family, of your own creating.

VIII.

DEFECTIVE POWERS.

Two females appeared before the bench.

Court: What is your demand?

Plaintiff: She borrowed of me a black silk cloak, and will not return it.

C.: Does she owe you any money?

P.: No.

C. [*to the defendant*] : Have you a cloak of hers?

Defendant: Yes.

C.: As the property is not yours, why do not you restore it?

D.: I should have sent it back, but I cannot spare it.

C.: What is it worth?

D.: I do not know.

C.: What would you give for it?

D.: I do not know.

C.: The cloak bears some value, and as you have long been in possession you must be apprised of that value. What is it likely to sell for?

D.: I cannot tell.

C.: As the plaintiff, out of friendship, has favoured you with it so long, and as you find it so extremely useful, you would have no objection to purchase it at an easy price, and pay the money when you are able; fix upon it, if you please, that easy price.

D.: I cannot.

Court [*to the plaintiff*] : We are sorry your honest property covered a cheat, and that the means of redress are not with us. We are not authorised to

go beyond matters of debt; this is an act of trover.
The cloak is probably pawned, or sold. Could we
have drawn a price from her we had stood upon firm
ground, and could have reduced your antagonist; but,
like an old bird of prey, she is too cunning to be
caught. You have lost your cloak, and she her
character, if she had one to lose. You are defrauded
under the mask of friendship. Of all the species of
ill-treatment that against good-nature is the least
pardonable. By a wistful look, you seem still to
wish our assistance; we would gladly give it. The
case is well understood; but, although it lies in a
narrow compass, our powers are too circumscribed to
reach it. We are obliged to dismiss the cause.

IX.

A B C.

THE world is a mask. He alone is fit for busy life
whose keen eye can see through the disguise. We
do wrong things, and call them by wrong names.
As I had no intention of writing down the trials, when
they happened, I have forgotten the names of the
parties; I must, therefore, supply their place with the
old-fashioned letters A B C, letters that often made us
sick in our childhood.

A poor widow sued A, who was a young woman
and a beauty. She pleaded her marriage, and that,
as a wife, she could not be sued.

It was proved upon the trial that she had been
under a contract of marriage to B, a young fellow.
They had been asked in the church, and had enjoyed

all the privileges of a husband and wife. Her charms, however, could not fix the rover. He wished to dispose of her to his friend C. As A and B had been recently asked in the church it was thought *that* asking would serve C and A, by which an expense of time and of money would be saved. C, therefore, in his own person, married her in the name of his friend B. C exactly followed the footsteps of his predecessor, enjoyed her, and left her. She was sued in the name of C.

The clerk of the Court and the Bench rather differed in opinion. He alleged that she had been really married, consequently was the wife of somebody; that the man to whom she was married must be her husband, and that a summons must issue against him.

Court: That she is not married to the man to whom she was asked in the church is plain, for he never appeared at the altar, nor did he commission any one to marry her by proxy, and we suppose, if *Madan* himself was upon the Bench, he would scarcely fix her upon him, for it does not appear this is her first connection. That the second is not her husband is as plain, for he put a trick upon the church by lending a person who had no business there, and by counterfeiting a name he had no right to use. This she connived at, for the shadow of a husband, a name precious beyond every name, to a girl of warm passions and of flimsy virtue. In the dear name *husband* is included every blessing till that husband is procured, and then every blessing is wanting. No banns had been published; if the register, which is the test of marriage, should be subsequently examined, the man at the altar could not be found in the book; and the

name found belonged to a person who was never there.
If a couple are not married according to law they are
not married at all. Though she is brought here in
the name of a husband we cannot consider her a wife,
therefore must dismiss the cause. Had she been sued
in her own name we could have proceeded with
safety.

X.

THE SERVANT AND HIS TWO MASTERS.

Two men, like two eyes, though differently situated,
point to the same object, self-interest. One man
hovers between right and wrong, without knowing
where to settle, till at last revenge preponderates the
balance; another seems satisfied if he can secure his
property upon a safer footing, although that security
is only imaginary; and a third, if he can ward off the
evil of the present day to a future; all act from this
motive, all deceive, and are deceived.

Hodgetts worked as a journeyman with Higgins,
ran forty-five shillings in his debt, and left him to
work with Meadows. Higgins applying for payment,
the three parties agreed that Meadows should stop two
shillings a week out of Hodgetts's wages till the debt
was discharged. Hodgetts left Meadows when he
had stopped eighteen shillings, which, instead of
giving to Higgins, Meadows paid back to Hodgetts.
This verifies the old adage, *Two of a trade dis-
agree.*

Higgins, ill-advised, sued Hodgetts for twenty-
seven shillings, and recovered. He then sued

Meadows for the eighteen. Meadows alleged he never promised Higgins payment, that he got nothing by the debt, and that he considered the money deposited in his hands as Hodgetts's property, for it had never changed its owner.

Court: When the agreement was made between the three parties it was only a bargain of honour. Hodgetts was not obliged to pay Meadows, Meadows could not compel him. Higgins could not oblige Meadows to pay, he had only made a conditional promise, for he could not tell whether Hodgetts would continue with him, or even live, or earn money enough to leave in his hands. Had that promise been positive, it would have bound Meadows. Higgins began at the wrong end of his work when he sued Hodgetts, for in him rested his whole security; in suing him for a part he has cut himself off from the remainder, if he miscarries in this suit with Meadows, for he cannot claim a second time upon Hodgetts. As Hodgetts consented to deposit the money in the hands of Meadows it was no longer his, he could not demand it back; Meadows could not detain it, it was not his. While Higgins is unsatisfied, it must be his property; and as Meadows held it by the consent of three parties for such a use, he cannot otherwise dispose of it without the consent of those three parties. If, in the interim, Hodgetts had paid the debt, or Higgins forgiven it, Higgins's title to the eighteen shillings would have ceased, and that title would again revive in Hodgetts. We must make an order against Meadows, and he will find his remedy against Hodgetts.

XI.

WARNING.

CUSTOM, by long practice, grows into a habit, and in time acquires the force of a law. It is then more tenaciously kept than the laws of a country; the reason is, that somebody has an interest in keeping it. If an ancient custom is good, it merits support; if bad, every means should be used to break it. Common justice is the touchstone by which it can be tried. No Court is more likely to determine between a good and a bad custom, to support the one, and abolish the other, than the Court of Conscience; because the chicanery of corrupt law is not admitted, and they have only common justice for their guide.

One, among many bad customs, is the *foot-ale*, practised by the lower class, which initiates the young beginner into the early habits of drinking. Another is the *garnish*, when a culprit enters confinement. If he has no money, his clothes have been stripped off his back; and though worth but little, have been sold for half their value, the money drank, and the prisoner left naked. The human brute, who performed this barbarous task, would, if not prevented by law, have stripped off his skin, could he have sold it for twopence.

Another is the *fees*, at quitting the prison. If a man offends, he offends against his country; that country is bound to procure a place of confinement. It is contrary to the idea of rectitude to force a man into a place, and then oblige him to pay for that place. If compulsion is used, he has no right to pay; if he pays, he has a right to choose his place. If he is

3

afterwards acquitted, punished, or pardoned, the law
is fully satisfied; his country has no more demand upon
him. It follows—the exaction of fees is a robbery,
but with this difference from his own: he perhaps has
robbed, and paid the penalty of the law; he is robbed,
but without redress. Garnish, and fees, with harpy
claws, have made many attempts to steal into the
prison belonging to this Court; but I am persuaded they
will never succeed during the power of the present
Commissioners.

The last I shall mention is the *harriot*; the
barbarous remains of Norman slavery. When a
customary tenant dies, the lord of the manor enters
the premises of the deceased, and seizes the best piece
of goods, quick or dead, he died possessed of. One
would think, from this cruel custom, our ancestors
were strangers to pity, or that the laws had lost their
protection. While the poor family are in the utmost
distress for the loss of their leader, an animal
approaches, in the form of a bailiff, with a heart as
callous as his who introduced the custom, and adds
to that distress by plundering their small remains of
property; he has been known to take an only cow,
which the deceased was supposed to have hastened his
death by labouring to purchase. The affliction
occasioned by one death, augmented by the seizure
of their best movable, is sufficient to cause another.
This vile custom originated from the Saxons, was
carried to its altitude by the Normans, and is part of
that wretched feudal system, which for many ages
disgraced humanity.

There are customs which time has not fully ascertained, but are yet wavering, and are complied with
or not, according to the honour, caprice, or conveniency

of the parties. Of this class is that of *warning* between master and servant.

A little smart girl of fourteen summoned her master.

Court: What is your claim.

Girl: Five shillings.

Master: I owe her nothing.

G.: It is for a month's wages at three pounds a year; he discharged me without warning.

M.: There was no agreement between us, either for wages or warning.

C.: For what reason did she quit?

M.: My wife and she had some words, and as I thought her impertinent I ordered her out of my house.

C.: And if you order every impertinent person out of your house, will there be anybody left in?

M.: She is something in my debt, for my wife furnished her with some trifles of wearing apparel, expecting she would stay, but as she does not, I expect to be paid for them.

Court: The question of warning has frequently come before us, and, as it appeared variously circumstanced, has been variously determined. It is not customary for the bricklayer, tailor, &c., to give or take warning; we do not enforce it because neither are disappointed. A master in the Birmingham trades has sometimes stopped his servant's wages for leaving him abruptly; but as warning, though perhaps eligible, was not practised, and as either side can generally supply the defect, we have not enforced it. But the case of servant girls in a family, like this before us, is different. Custom has in some degree introduced it, and common justice ratified it. We do not much enquire whether it was part of the original contract; we suppose it to exist. If the maid was allowed to quit her service at a moment's notice, how could the business of a family be conducted? Without the laborious hand matters would quickly run into con-fusion. The mistress perhaps might attempt to do what she is unable, and much would be left undone. Her necessity would force her to make a speedier choice than her prudence. She might find, to her sorrow, she had changed a bad servant for a worse, which brings her into the same situation, to the injury of herself, and disparagement of her place, in a fortnight.

Again, if the mistress could instantly discharge the maid, how could the maid subsist till another place offers? Necessity, in all probability, would put her upon dishonourable means to live, the least of which is contracting a debt never to be paid. By a habit of idleness, she may be thrown into the arms of a man she would otherwise reject; if not, prostitution may follow, or, what is worse, theft. Loss of character shuts up every place against her, and opens the prospect of a miserable end.

But reasonable as warning appears, there are cases where it ought to be dispensed with, as, when a girl is famished, beaten, or otherwise cruelly treated. On the other hand, the mistress may instantly discharge the maid if she is caught in an indecent act, keeps bad hours, becomes pregnant, is guilty of pilfering, &c.

In common cases, if the maid quits her place, the mistress has a right to a month's wages; if the mistress discharges her the girl has the same demand, and this seems the case before us.

With regard to any little matters of perquisite received by the girl, if they were lent, they must be returned; if sold, paid for; but if given, as these probably were, they cannot be demanded back; whatever is given us, we have an absolute right to. We must, therefore, make an order in favour of the girl.

SECOND EXAMPLE.

A servant maid quitting her place, the mistress desired her to recommend another. She communicated this intelligence to a young woman at Dudley, who came over, underwent the usual examination, was approved, entertained at three pounds per annum and was ordered to deposit her apparel in her future bedroom.

While this was transacting, the old servant, hurt, when the moment of separation came, at the idea of being supplanted, hinted to the mistress her wish to stay, which was complied with, and the Dudley girl, when she came down stairs, was given to understand there would be no need of her service, and she might immediately depart. She sued for a month's wages. The Court observed that the girl could make no claim for travelling from Dudley, that uncertain journey arose from her own choice, and must be supported at her own expense, in which the mistress had no concern; nor could she claim if the mistress and she had disagreed. But the moment one was taken into the service of the other they were as much mistress and servant as if they had been together a year. The bargain was fairly made, and must be fairly dissolved.

The mistress exclaimed loudly against the injustice of the Court. "They might as well pick her pocket as oblige her to pay for service never done, and that she neither agreed for wages or warning." The Court entered an order against her with this remark: If the girl had voluntarily quitted your service after the agreement was made, and her clothes deposited, we should have obliged her to pay you a month's wages; it follows, she ought to be paid.

THIRD EXAMPLE.

After the experience of two days between a mistress and her maid, it appeared they could no more agree together than fire and water. "We will separate," says the mistress. "Then I will have a month's wages," replied the maid, "for the Court will allow it." "If you insist upon the money," says the other, "you shall earn it by serving the month. Clean the dairy." "I will not," she answered, and sat down to sleep, even in a storm.

Nine days elapsed, as boisterous as those in November, when the master offered the girl four shillings, which was rejected, and discharged her. She sued for the month.

The Court remarked, a servant refusing to do what was ordered might not always arise from disobedience, for a mistress might command her to two employments at the same time, while she could not perform more than one; but if she is to be paid and maintained it is requisite, however, she should perform that one. A girl cannot claim for a month except she labours that month. If she has a right to the master's money, he has a right to her service. As she did not choose to work we do not choose to give her more than the master offered, and as the master made the tender the expense of the suit falls upon her.

Fourth Example.

The master of a public house sued a youth for nineteen shillings. He allowed the debt. But having married a girl, who had lived seven months in service with the master, she charged him with a debt of eleven shillings; six of which were wages unpaid—she alleging their agreement was for three pounds a year, and he only fifty shillings—and five for the month, she being instantly discharged. The parties grew violent. He treated her as a cheat, and she boldly charged him with having an amour with two or three of his servant girls, whom she named. The crowd enjoyed a real laugh at his expense, and he joined them with a forced one. The Court reprimanded her for revealing secrets which had no business there, and asked whether his greatest crime might not consist in neglecting her? They further enquired, For what reason was she discharged? She replied, she accidentally caught her mistress in bed with another man, and published it.

Court: If you were caught in the same situation would you wish it published? You acted against yourself, for while you kept a secret which hurt nobody, you made your mistress your servant; when you divulged it, you made her your enemy. You stood a fairer chance to cure the evil by silence than by promulgation. Whatever servant betrays the important secrets of a family betrays a trust which is highly culpable. Even truth itself must not always be told. Should every person's private transactions be laid open to the world such a scene of confusion would follow as never appeared since the days of Adam, that of the Flood not excepted, for it would overwhelm the *whole* race; there could not be found even eight persons so fortunate as to escape the deluge. A man, conscious of innumerable errors, would be ashamed to be seen in the street—No, he might safely venture there, for none would be found to see him.

Whether the wages were fifty shillings or three pounds is not proved by either. This point, therefore, must be determined by our own judgment. As you seem by appearance to merit three pounds, we shall allow it; but as you did not merit the month's wages, we shall not. Your mistress has a greater right to discharge you instantly than you to demand the money. Though she was caught in a crime, her punishment was not with you. No servant is to injure the family in which he resides. The mistress has lost more by your tongue than she can gain by your five shillings.

XII.

THE MEEK HUSBAND AND THE BOUNCING WIFE.

A MAN tinctured with idleness, and a woman with pride, attempt, like the spider, to feed on the vitals of others. There are two ways in Birmingham of supporting the necessitous—the contributions of the parish, and those of the sick clubs, which are numerous. The support of luxury is not to be expected from either. It is a burlesque upon charity to maintain people in affluence with money drawn from the pockets of those who are but just above want themselves; this is a kind of legal robbery. A reform is wanting, when the receiver fares better than the giver.

T. had long been member of a sick club; had long hung upon the box, and, though a young man, seemed inclinable to hang for life. The club, considering him an impostor, and frightened at his being entailed on them for ever, withheld the pay.

Not a Court day passes without some club causes coming before the Bench; all consist of those who are willing to receive, but unwilling to pay; among others came the humble T. with his showy lady. The Commissioners, from the appearance of his face, which is an index that points to the state of the body, as well as the mind, and from a certificate written by a gentleman of the faculty, made an order in his favour.

Elated with this success, madam bullied the members, who in turn were determined to be rid of T., and endeavoured to omit receiving his weekly contribution to the club, that by six weeks' omission he might forfeit his right to membership; but the Court would not allow of any finesse.

T., or rather his wife, frequently brought the stewards to the Court. The Commissioners particularly enquired into his complaint. She was the speaker; he was composed of humility, and never opened his mouth but by her order. No material defect was exhibited, and madam seemed rather to lose ground. The cause was continued for proof. Every means was tried in the interim to induce the Bench to give judgment in her favour. The overseers stepped forward. Some of the faculty used their interest, which, as it was granting a favour to him, might be paid for by her. She even applied individually to the Commissioners, and stated that she had *only* sixteen shillings a week coming in, seven from the club, five from the parish, and four from another quarter; that she could not subsist upon it; that she expected to be aided in acquiring more, rather than be deprived of this.

The Commissioners were surprised at the sixteen shillings a week, besides being possessed of a husband, who seemed able to labour, but afraid to be well. They replied, a cause seems too bad to support itself that requires so much trouble to support it; that they were neuter in the case, that the matter would be tried by the laws of the club, by which she must stand or fall, and that they were not dealers in favour, by justice.

At the trial madam appeared all noisy, her husband all silence; if the club was loud, she was louder. The Bench frequently attempted to silence her, but they could as soon have silenced a pig under the butcher's knife. Their articles were produced, in which was one expressly declaring, "If a member was deemed an impostor, by any surgeon, he should be expelled the society." Two of the faculty were present; one pronounced, "he was well able to work"; the other, "that though he had a slight rupture, it was very little impediment."

Court: We have given the case great attention. We have tried it by our own judgment, and by your laws. There is no reason why men, who can barely support themselves, should support others equally able. We shall dismiss the cause.

Madam opened—thunder was discharged from her tongue, and lightning from her eyes. Her face—round, red, and fiery, like a rising full moon in a clear winter's night, looked sufficiently heated to kindle a match. She surveyed the Bench as the Dragon of Wantley did Moore of Moorehall.

As I well knew T. I could observe that, being deprived of the box, he immediately changed his dress, discharged the air of sickness from his face, assumed a brisker gait, and turned his hand to labour. He appeared as much in health as other people. His countenance being rather pale, might be the case of any man possessed of a rampant wife.

XIII.

THE LOVERS.

WE live upon the most intimate terms of friendship with another, we mix our property with his, we form in our minds an everlasting union, and fondly hope the happy season will never change. But ere long the day lours, the clouds thicken, and the jarring elements proclaim an inveterate war. If everything is subject to change, love and friendship cannot be exempt. The closer the union, the wider the difference. There was a time when each kept the other's secrets, but now they are blazoned in the strongest light.

A decent girl sued a young fellow for one pound, nineteen shillings, and elevenpence.

Defendant: I owe her nothing.

Court: What is the nature of the debt?

Girl: It was money he received of me.

D. : I did not borrow it; she gave it me.

C. : You seem to have been upon better terms than at present; perhaps you had love in possession, and wedlock in prospect.

D. : She wanted me to marry her.

C. : And you wanted to rob *her*.

D. : She gave me the money, and everything she could give beside—(with a significant smile).

C. : Then she gave you what you did not deserve. If you have taken what you cannot restore, you ought to restore what you can. He who betrays his friend acts beneath the character of a man; what then does he deserve who, without any motive but revenge, divulges in public what ought to be kept inviolate? If your accusations fall heavy upon her, they fall with double weight upon yourself. Having no character of your own to destroy, you destroy another's. Instead of associating with women you ought even to be hissed out of the company of men; you have inverted the old adage, " A woman's a riddle, and can keep nothing." But it is in vain to cut the man without feeling. She parted with her money in confidence of a marriage, in which case it would still have been her own; for whatever belongs to the one belongs to the other; but this marriage not taking effect, and she may rejoice it did not, she still retains a right to the property. She was in your power, and you acted the wanton tyrant; we shall put you in hers by ordering a speedy payment.

XIV.

LANDLORD AND TENANT.

It is entertaining to contemplate the graduation of things; to behold a first cause, of no moment, produce a second, that second produce a good, that good an evil, and that evil a remedy: every link in the chain of events draws forward, and terminates in the next.

The manufactures of Birmingham require an amazing number of people to conduct them, and though their wages are from ten shillings a week to two guineas, yet they are as poor as the common labourer, who earns but eight. Imprudence is the characteristic of this class. The few that are otherwise soon become masters, and rise to fortune. This prodigious number of the lower ranks require a proportionate number of small houses for their accommodation. With these we abound. The landlords can readily let their houses, but they loudly complain their rents are ill paid. The man who melts down his weekly income has but little left, besides promises, for his landlord. A distress cannot be taken, the effects would not pay the charge. Riches are said to give power, but here the case is reversed, for the poverty of the tenant is his security, and gives him a power over the landlord. Of all the men we contend with, he is the hardest to conquer who has nothing to lose. The laws of England point out but one way to recover the landlord's premises, by eject-ment, and this he dares not pursue; the whole expense would fall upon himself, besides having the wretched chance of placing them in the hands of another of the same stamp. After he has experienced evil upon evil, without a cure, he flies for relief to the Court of Requests. In this Court, if properly authorised, a man might find that universal nostrum for his property, which is vainly held forth by the faculty, for his health.

Court: What is your demand?

Landlord: As much as the Court can allow. He is my tenant, and will neither pay rent, nor quit the place. I would forgive the debt if he would grant possession.

C.: Why do not you pay the rent?

Tenant: I have no money.

C.: Why do not you quit the house?

T.: I cannot get another.

C.: By not paying rent you act against yourself. No landlord will let you a house that knows it. Can a man lay out his money in purchase, submit to repairs, discharge parliamentary taxes, and have no returns? We live *by* one another, and it is requisite we should, but we are not to live *upon* another. If you will quit the premises directly, you shall have your own time to discharge the debt; if not, we will make an order for immediate payment, in which case you will instantly be committed to prison.

T.: Give me one week, and I will quit.

C.: You shall have it.—There are [*to the landlord*] three ways before us. If you can take your tenant's word, we can make an order in small payments, which will favour him; if not, we can continue the cause a week, for sixpence, to see if he fulfils his promise; or we can make an immediate order for the whole, but in this last case you must give *your* promise that you will not hurt him if he performs his.

L.: I will take his word.

Second Example.

Taylor, a gay young fellow, rented a workshop of Edmunds, an industrious young widow. She wanting the shop, desired him to quit, which he refusing, she sent him a written order to leave the premises, in three months, or pay double rent. This order being disregarded, she brought him to the Court.

He alleged, " as he had fairly taken the premises, he had a right to keep them; and as they had both agreed for simple rent, it could not be altered without him."—It was replied that she having full power over the shop, had granted a participation of that power, by admitting him tenant at will. Had he possessed a lease he might have enjoyed all its privileges during the term, but being only a temporary tenant he could possess only a temporary privilege. He could not hold more than was granted, otherwise he would hold the property of another, and she lose the authority of an owner.—The Court asked their clerk whether a landlord could legally charge double rent; who assured them an Act for that purpose existed, and its intent was to prevent the dreadful expense of ejectments. The Court then remarked, as legal notice had been fairly proved, and as possession ought to have been delivered up at the end of that notice, they should make an order for the rent demanded.

The tenant and his attorney became violent. " The premises should never be delivered up; they were suitable; the decision was unjust; and a remedy would be found in law."—But I have long observed, he who threatens to do most, does nothing.—The tenant asked the Court whether he could continue possession under the double rent awarded?

Court: It is not our province to solve doubtful points of law; we leave them to the long-robe; but we apprehend she may, after legal notice, still double her demands. If you reflect a moment, you fall by your own argument; "you will not part with the shop, because it is useful"; you forget the same reason operates with her, but with double force, because she has a right, and you have not. Should the cause come again before us, you may expect the harshest sentence ever awarded by this Court; for we deem it a fundamental maxim, if one man holds the property of another against his consent, has power to restore it, and will not, he ought to be punished till he will.

XV.

QUEER ASPECTS.

CAN you, my dear reader, form an idea how a man looks who is possessed of the harshest features that ever compose a face, and who expects to win a cause and twenty-four shillings, both which are his right, but wins neither? or, how two hundred people, assembled in a public Court, look upon a man who had rather have some of the blackest crimes held up to view, with death annexed, than pay a just debt of twenty-four shillings, although he is well able? Or how even a Commissioner looks, who attempts to lead others, when he is lost himself; instead of *being a guide*, wants one? If you can, you will form so just an idea of the following case as may save you the trouble of reading it.

Shad sued P. September 1, 1785, for one pound four shillings. P. acknowledged the debt might have been contracted, but pleaded the statute of limitations, which annihilates a debt after a lapse of six years, provided that debt is not kept alive by a continued account between the parties, or by an acknowledgment, or a promise from the debtor. Shad declared he had had a running account, had recently sold him goods, and received payment. The Court continued the cause, and desired him to produce his books the next Court-day.

It appeared the debt sued for was contracted in 1778, after which P. went into the army, and was absent five years. At his return he frequently bought shoes of Shad, had not much credit, and had since paid.

The question to be considered by the Commissioners was, Whether the new connection preserved the old debt? It was argued in favour of the delinquent that the old demand stood by itself, stands the same still, and is cured by time; that whatever P. bought he paid for. That as P. out of gratitude had become a customer again, it would be ungenerous to trap him for conferring those favours upon Shad, which he might have conferred upon another.

It was urged in reply that P. laid himself open to a suit by appearing in the verge of the Court within six years. That his becoming a customer might excite Shad's patience, who might otherwise have made a more early attack; that the Commissioners did not conceive they had any right to destroy a debt; that a new debt will piece to an old one, as well at the end of five years as five days; and, as the two debts did not seem divided, either by time, law, or reason, they must consider them as one.

The Bench having got over this stumbling-block, fell upon a greater. It was pleaded *in favour of P.*

4

that in the five years above mentioned, he had been condemned in a Court of justice for housebreaking; that his father, by his prudent behaviour, as sergeant in the Militia, had obtained the good graces of Lord B., his colonel, by whose interest he had procured a pardon for the son, who had since settled, become a master, lived in credit, and stood a fair chance of acquiring a fortune.   That the moment sentence of death is passed upon a man he is dead in law; the Judge can order instant execution. He can make no will, he can bequeath no effects, he can inherit no property, nor transact any business with the living. No action can lie against him; all his own debts are cut off, no creditor can claim upon him; consequently this demand ceases; and this is the practice of all our Courts.

But it was remarked, if the law killed, the Crown could make alive; that a pardon reinstated a man where the law found him. If the Crown gives life, it gives all its appendages; everything belonging to the man revives with him, consequently his debts. If he can claim, as P. had done, why not pay? The Crown is defective if it cannot do what the law has undone. And to suppose life restored without action is to suppose an impossibility.

These reasons operated with the Bench, but still there was an obstacle they could not surmount, the practice of all the Courts; which they were assured, by professional men, existed.   The Commissioners were set fast.   They found themselves completely hemmed in between law and equity, and like Sterne's starling, "they could not get out." If they attempted one side, they would fly in the face of law; if the other, they would break the bounds of equity; all the quirks of Westminster Hall could not relieve them.—That the debt was due to Shad did not admit a doubt, but how to give it him did.

As the whole legislative power is in the hands of the King, lords, and commons, and as every act of theirs is supposed the act of every man in the kingdom, it becomes requisite to pay a deference to the laws, though they may not exactly hit our sentiments. He pays his country an ill compliment who sets up his private judgment against theirs; besides, the precedent is dangerous; for if a man can trample upon one law, why not another, which would immediately put a period to government? If a man will not submit to the laws, because those laws are defective, there is an end of submission, for no perfect system can exist, the weakness of our nature will not allow it. Again, if the Commissioners acted against law, they acted against an authority equal to that under which they sat; for the same powers which favoured the culprit constituted them a Bench. Two evils offered, one of which they were obliged to commit; they therefore chose what they conceived to be the least, that of dismissing the cause. If they had acted against law, they could not have made reparation; but by giving it a simple dismission they left Shad at liberty to pursue his antagonist in another Court, or even in this, if any further light could be thrown on the subject.

The suitors were both hurt; one because he could not recover his property, and the other because the noisome snuff, which had been extinguished by a pardon, was publicly lighted up in Court.

XVI.

THE PRIVILEGE OF A COCKADE.

JUSTICE, like physic, will not take effect on every subject, nor the attempt to cure answer the expense.—A plaintiff demanded a guinea. The Court asked the defendant if it was right.

Defendant: I am a soldier, an't please your honour.

Court: We claim no honour, nor you neither, if you refuse paying your debts. If you owe the money, you can make no objection to pay it.

D.: I owe the money, your honour, but I serve the king.

C.: But you do not serve his subjects while you defraud them of their property. We often complain, and with reason, against people who serve the king.—We can enter an order in your favour [*to the plaintiff*] as in other cases; we could issue an execution against his goods, with effect, but he has none. We can instantly seize his body, but we cannot hold it; his officer will demand him out of our hands. He is a bird of passage, and to shoot flying will scarcely pay for powder and shot. You are pursuing an *ignis fatuus*, which will lead into a slough—the more you struggle, the deeper you sink. All you can gain by this suit is to perpetuate the debt. It will survive the wreck of six years; it cannot slip through the fingers of time; but if he ever procures a discharge, and is found within the precincts of the Court, you may commit everything to prison, but his honour.

XVII.

THE POWER OF BEAUTY.

PERFECTION is not with us.   The best institution has
its errors.   The brightest gem may have a flaw.
Judgment is random, and a trial a chance.   Equity
appears in such a variety of character, she is not
known.   There are many ways of losing a cause
which she never travels.   Thomas Parker, ancestor to
the present Lord Macclesfield, who, by his shining
talents at the Bar, raised his family to the peerage, when
asked, in the reign of Queen Anne, why he gained a
cause for the plaintiff at one assize, and for the
defendant the next, replied, "I was better fee'd, and
better informed."   Here equity was out of the question;
the silver tongue and the golden fleece commanded the
prize.

An unaccountable prejudice will take possession of
the heart of a Judge, almost unobserved by himself,
and preponderate the scale in favour of one side.   My
dear reader, you never saw two people fight, but you
threw your good wishes into the ring, upon one of the
combatants, although equally a stranger to both, and
the merits of their quarrel.   The weaker the man, the
stronger his prepossession.

The deficiency of human judgment is another
fountain of error; but here the Judge stands excused;
no man can act beyond his power.

Misinformation is another force of evil; both parties
equally treat him with deceit.   The only people who
can throw light upon the subject will not.   As they

keep him in the dark, if he blindly distributes the gifts
of fortune, the fault is more theirs than his own.

It is difficult not to be won by the first speaker,
if he carries the air of mildness, and is master of his
tale; or not to be biased in favour of infirmity, or of
infancy. Those who cannot assist themselves we are
much inclined to assist.

Nothing dissolves like tears. Though they arise
from weakness, they are powerful advocates, which
instantly disarm, particularly those which the afflicted
wish to hide. They come from the heart, and will
reach it, if the Judge has a heart to reach. Distress
and pity are inseparable. The man who can repel
fire and sword is reduced by a few drops of water.

Perhaps there never was a Judge, from seventeen
to seventy, who could look with indifference upon
beauty in distress; if he could, he was unfit to be a
Judge. Though these masterly drawings of nature
chiefly strike those in younger life, yet none are
exempt. He should be a stranger to decision who is
a stranger to compassion. All these matters influence
the man, and warp his judgment.

Kirtland having occasion to pay one pound twelve
shillings to a person at Willenhall, for goods bought,
applied to the carrier's inn, and saw, in the same
figure, a beauty, and a landlady. "She could receive
anything." Perhaps the reader may object to a
union of the words *beauty* and *landlady*, and think the
first ought to be expunged by an erratum, and *bulky*,
the usual companion of landlady, inserted in its room;
but however seldom the two first assimilate, he must
for this once allow them to pass. He delivered the
money to her, wrapped in a paper, and directed, told
her the sum, and for whom. She deposited it in a

corner cupboard, where she observed, "It would be safe till the carrier came."

After some months had elapsed, the person at Willenhall wrote for his money, which brought on an enquiry. Kirtland was obliged to send a second one pound twelve shillings, and recover the first how he could. After many fruitless applications, he brought her to the Court. A man of moderate intellects is scarcely a match, in a disputable point, for a woman that is young, handsome, and can speak well; the disproportion is still greater if she can enlist under her banner those who have talents and power.—The Bench was uncommonly crowded, chiefly with Commissioners not used to attend business, who, retreating when the trial was over, gave reason to think this was the principal cause.

It was pleaded in her favour that she was in a distressed situation; that she ought not to be responsible, because she could receive no profit from the money; that in the act of receiving and delivering goods she could be considered in no other light than the carrier's servant; and that application ought to be made to the master for repayment.

It was observed in reply that the carrier had declined business, and was a resident in Willenhall, consequently out of the reach of the Court; that application had been made to him, who answered, "He knew nothing of the matter"; which gave reason to suspect the money had been applied to another use. If she had said, You may leave the property, if you please, but I will not take charge of it, she had been clear, but her accepting the money was accepting a responsibility. She did not receive it as a servant; Kirtland can look to none but her. She must either return the money, or prove its delivery to the carrier. If this doctrine is not allowed, a man's property cannot be safe. Kirtland has no claim upon the carrier, except she fixes one for him, and if she pays the money, she can fix one for herself. However the Commissioners might vary in opinion, yet, on which side right lay, must be decided by the grandest tribunal upon earth, that of the public. The Bench, by a majority, gave it in favour of the landlady, and Kirtland for ever lost his money.

XVIII.

THE HUNDRED-POUND NOTE.

Some faults merit the rod, others are too great for punishment. If the rude lad breaks his tea-cup, a flogging may settle accounts between him and mamma; but if he overturns the whole tea-equipage, astonishment seizes the family, and, through the greatness of the crime, the delinquent escapes.

The arts of stamping and refining metals have of late years been carried to great perfection, and have well paid the artist. M. thought if he could acquire these enriching powers he should at least be possessed of a second-hand philosopher's stone, which, if it could not convert everything to gold, would extract silver out of even dirt and iron.

He engaged Baylis, a simple fellow, who was a hired servant to a refiner. The refiner, provoked at being tricked out of his trade and his servant, brought a warrant for Baylis, and sent him to prison, and an action against M. which produced a trial at Warwick

Assizes. The refiner won the cause, but a man wins nothing if his antagonist has nothing to lose. During the dull process of law M. had acquired all he wanted from Baylis, and, like his master, discarded him. He afterwards brought him to the Court of Requests. M. not chosing to appear himself, sent his wife.

Court: What is your claim?

Wife: One pound sixteen.

C.: Do you allow the debt?

Baylis: No, I owe nothing.

C.: How do you establish your demand?

W.: It is part of a larger debt, for which I hold his note.

C.: Where is the note?

W.: In my pocket.

C.: Produce it.

It appeared to be a promissory note, plentifully worded by an attorney, upon a sixpenny stamp, for one hundred pounds, payable at three shillings a week; twelve were elapsed. This was obtained from Baylis's simplicity to bind him to M. without any value given, except what was spent in prison, and except a promise that M. would find him employment for seven years, at twenty-four shillings per week; but it appeared he was unable to perform that promise, had it been but for seven weeks.

C.: Were you in liquor when you gave this note?

B.: No.

C.: Were you in your senses?—You may safely answer No to that question.—How can you [*to the wife*] justify persuading a 100*l.* note out of an ignorant man, for which you gave no value? You might as well, while you were drawing it, have inserted a 1,000; one would have been paid as soon as the other, for they would both lie till the day of general retribution.

W.: What must I do with the note?

C.: Light your pipe with it. Had the debt been just, you displayed a weakness in taking a 100*l.* note from an imprudent journeyman, not worth a shilling, and encumbered with four small children. If the demand was fair, and he an economist, twenty generations of Commissioners would fall a prey to time, and Baylis himself must live to the age of Methusalem, before he could discharge it. There would be no more chance of its being paid than the web of a spider, or the good-nature of an old maid, lasting to eternity. But we are inclined to think the names in the note should have been reversed, for as he has been a loser by you, and you a gainer by him, you ought rather to have given *him* a 100*l.* note, which by the way would have been as valid as this. Had the note been for *shillings* instead of pounds it might have passed the Bench unnoticed, for we generally pay attention to a man's writing; it is a stronger evidence than his word; but as we conceive so pompous a thing as a 100*l.* note, though a plaything with him, is above our reach, we shall dismiss the cause, set the delinquent free, and leave this short lesson with you: That a man's hired servant is as much his property as the tools in his shop, and that a note obtained like this will neither add to your credit nor fortune.

The Second Part of the Hundred-Pound Note.

A few weeks after, M. brought again to the Court his antagonist, his note, and his attorney. The same arguments paced it again, over the same ground. No

new incidents arising, the Court saw no reason to alter
their sentiments, and were giving the cause a second
dismission, not from the size of the note, for had it
been just he had a right to choose what mode of
recovery he pleased, when the attorney desired a continuance till the next Court-day, which was granted.
In the interim the action, which promised no success,
was withdrawn, and Baylis arrested for twelve pounds.

The random Baylis was terrified at the sight of a
prison where he had recently suffered, and knew he
could not find bail to keep himself out; M. foresaw a
certain expense in pursuing a pauper, and that his
flimsy sixpenny stamp would not bear the keen eye
of a Court of justice; these considerations produced
an agreement, which was that the 100*l.* note should
be cancelled, and another given of forty, payable by
two shillings a week. Thus the simple Baylis riveted
those chains upon himself which his enemy could not
hang on.

When a small part of this 40*l.* note became due,
M. again tried his fortune in the Court, urged every
argument that could be suggested by his attorney and
himself, to induce the Bench to give judgment in his
favour, but the note was rejected with these remarks:
That the first note was unfairly obtained, no value
being given; that if M. was the cause of the other
being sent to prison, he ought to support him there;
a soldier is not sent to war at his own expense; that
he had been a gainer by Baylis, in acquiring a trade,
but the other had been no gainer by him; that one of
the terms of agreement for the first note was that M.
should give him twenty-four shillings per week for
seven years; this was not performed, consequently he
broke his part of the bargain, therefore could not

expect Baylis to perform his; and that the second note being founded on the first, was of the same nature: if one was bad, the other must be so too; if the foundation is rotten, the superstructure cannot be sound.

XIX.

THE MERCHANT AND THE BUTTON-MAKER.

Two long-winded combatants, like Broughton and Slack, may perpetuate a contest till they tire the spectators, and raise disputes among the Judges, without tiring themselves. There are questions that will bear an eternal wrangle, and there are stubborn tempers that will eternally wrangle upon them. Though the Bench frequently determine a hundred causes in two hours, yet they were now staggered with only one, but it was beyond the human powers to ascertain, and had, by fresh summonses, continuations, dismissions, and decisions, come before them about seven times, and must have taken up more than a whole day in discussion, and, after all, had left the Commissioners and both the parties dissatisfied.

A button-maker sued a merchant for 1*l.* 19*s.* 11*d.*, but remarked the debt was above four pounds. The merchant alleged he was thirteen and sevenpence in *his* debt. Each of them produced a bundle of papers to justify his claim; supported his demand with positive assertions, backed with some ill-nature. The Bench could not enter deeply into intricate accounts, and private memorandums understood by none but the makers. Each talked mighty loud, was mighty right, and awaked those errors in each other's life which had slumbered for twenty years. Both dealt in contradiction and scandal, but neither could bear them. Like Ætna and Vesuvius, they bellowed against each other in thunder, smoke, and fire. The Commissioners themselves could not escape being singed by the heat, for they were severally charged with giving a private audience to the enemy.

A man may dive deep and long before he finds a bottom where there is none. The Commissioners, however, could clearly discover there was money due to the button-maker; but as a counterbalance the merchant produced something like an ass-load of buttons that were defective, and returned as unfit for sale; these he would have sent back to the maker, but he could not be found, for being under a cloud, he had taken shelter in retreat.

The button-maker replied that no tradesman ought to take goods after being detained six months.—The Commissioners, as in duty bound, repeatedly fingered the buttons, which were as tractable as if under the command of Breslau, for they tumbled to pieces at a touch, but they could not, like him, make them whole. The Bench were divided in opinion, as men frequently are in disputable points, though they were well acquainted with the character of both parties.

First Commissioner: There seems to be something due to the button-maker.

Second Com.: If a manufacturer sends in bad goods the merchant has an option to keep or return them; if he does the latter, it ought to be directly—no man can justify keeping them six months; it is contrary to every rule of commerce; it deprives the maker of the opportunity of disposing of them elsewhere. If the buyer has a right to keep them six months, why not six years? which would give a fatal blow to trade.   By keeping them he makes them his own, therefore my voice shall unalterably go for the button-maker to have his money.

Third Com. : We have attended to this intricate case by the hour, and if we attend to it by the year we must at last give an uncertain decision, for we cannot penetrate to the bottom.   There is a loss, and as we know not the amount, nor who caused it, we know not how to fix it.   This loss must be borne by one or both of the parties; but both withdraw the shoulder from the burden.   There are two material questions for our consideration before we decide; whether the buttons are marketable? and if they are not, what time the merchant may fairly keep them?

That they are not marketable is evident even to us, who cannot see with the curious eye of a button-maker. All allow it but the maker himself; it follows that he is the first aggressor, the whole of this misunderstanding originates from him; the merchant is passive; and shall we, who ought to be guided by equity, punish one man for the faults of another?   A pattern-card is delivered to the merchant of the button and the price, and though not a word is spoken, it contains a tacit agreement that the goods shall be equal, or very near the pattern; if they are not, it is a deception arising from the maker, who alone ought to suffer.   If he is a man of honour he will take care to prevent it; but if they slip his attention that honour will oblige him to take them again.   To decide in favour of the button-maker would encourage the manufacture of a bad article, cast a stigma on the place where they rise, and tend to remove that manufacture to another, where it shall be better performed.   It would operate against

that country, for which we ought to entertain the most
sincere regard. Bad work tends, as it ought, to ruin
the maker; but it tends, as it ought not, to ruin the
merchant, by depriving him of the sale of his goods,
of his profits, his character, and brings him into the
high road to destruction. Common justice directs that
we should exert every method to prevent the circula-
tion of a ruinous article. The buttons before us will
not answer the end for which they were made; they
are not worth joining to a coat; he who sells them,
sells his customer. As the merchant had no hand in
their production he ought to have none in their loss;
consequently he stands clear of the first question.

What time a purchaser may fairly detain defective
goods cannot exactly be ascertained; it will vary with
circumstances, and here we must call in the aid of our
reason. We are not to suppose the man who buys
a hat can return it after having kept it half a year; he
might have discovered its errors sooner. If the shoes
pinch he may feel them on Sunday morning, and may
return them on Monday. If he finds a hole in his
stocking he must convey them back in a short space,
or the hosier may fairly suspect he has worn it. If
the auctioneer advertises that the goods shall be cleared
away with all their faults, no complaint of the buyer,
though made within an hour after purchase, can avail;
it was an agreement between them. But if the
auctioneer marks a piece of cloth twenty-five yards,
which measures but twenty, the buyer has his remedy,
because the auctioneer has broken his agreement; but
this remedy must be applied in a day or two, otherwise
the loss may fall on a wrong person; besides, even in
that time, the buyer has an opportunity of discovering
the mistake; nay, the very article before us may be

kept various lengths of time with propriety.   If I order
a set of buttons for a suit, and do not discover their
faults, and return them in a few days, I have no right
to return them at all, because the neglect is mine; I
have had full time, and I have no right to sport with
the property of another.   But though the article is the
same, the reasons widely differ.   These buttons were
delivered to the merchant packed in papers, with one
on the outside to shew the pattern.   It is expected by
all parties that those within are equal to that without;
but this cannot be discovered by the merchant; it is
not possible for him to open every parcel that comes
to his warehouse; he had better give up his profit and
his profession; consequently there is a necessary, an
unavoidable confidence reposed in the maker, a confidence that should be preserved inviolate; and shall
we assist in destroying it?   These goods, with a
variety of others, are deposited in casks, and shipped
to foreign parts; perhaps they went to Ireland, for we
know the merchant before us deals there.   How then
is it possible their quality should be known till they are
opened for retail use? and how can six months be an
unreasonable time?   The merchant and the purchaser's
right of returning is preserved by the faith of the
maker; his responsibility goes along with them till they
arrive at the consumer.   If this was not the case a
manufacturer might wrap up a log of timber instead
of a gross of buttons, and stand clear of mischief; nay,
what difference is there between a brick-end and a
button unfit for use?   The nature of the crime is the
same; it only differs in degree.   We cannot proceed
upon firmer ground than the general practice between
the maker and the merchant, that all goods of defective
quality may be returned, provided they are not

wantonly or *negligently* kept. I know a lot of goods are now returning from America for the maker. The length of time must, in some measure, depend upon the place to which they are sent; nay, I will go further, it is doubtful whether any given time can annihilate restitution for fraud. While the merchant has no chance of justifying himself, the maker must be his security. But whether the merchant is indebted to the button-maker, or the button-maker to him, is uncertain.

First Com.: Give the button-maker something.

Second Com.: I will not recede from my first resolution.

Third Com.: If the decision was vested in me I would give him a shilling, not so much because it is his due, as to put an end to the contest.

Button-maker: The whole is my due, and I will not take a farthing less. If you deprive me of this I will seek a remedy in another Court.

Merchant: I shall think you use me very ill if you oblige me to pay money to a man who owes me thirteen shillings and sevenpence.

Third Com.: The Bench is divided against itself, and their judgment cannot stand. The sense of those off the Bench is equally divided. We can neither decide to satisfy them nor ourselves; the sore is too much inflamed to admit a healing remedy. I will, if you choose, simply dismiss the cause, and leave the combatants to rake each other's vitals in a Court of law; plentiful bleeding will reduce the most fiery temper.

Second Com.: I will not consent to a dismission.

Third Com.: But if we cannot agree upon a judgment the cause dismisses itself. I will, if you please, enter a dismission after full hearing, which amounts to a determination, and excludes a cause from this Court, and every other, except the Lords.

Second Com. : I will not consent to that; the button-maker ought to have his money.

Third Com. : We row the cause from side to side, but the stubborn bank will not give way.

After much altercation, and two hours spent in this crabbed cause, it was determined to award the button-maker a guinea, to the dissatisfaction of every member.

XX.

THE FEE.

"WHERE no work is done, no money can be demanded," is a proverb which has stood the test of ages; and, though we cannot always adopt it, is founded in reason. If he who labours ought to be rewarded, it follows he who neglects ought not.

It is a received opinion that no class of people are better paid for their work than the gentlemen of the faculty and the law. This would be true if they could recover their money. Six months' credit is a rule of trade, but the rule of law and physic is apt to run six years. It is easy for a man to place a fortune in his books; the difficulty lies in getting it out. I am well acquainted with an attorney who, in the course of twenty years, deposited four thousand pounds in his journal, which arose from beggarly contests, not one of which, perhaps, will ever be paid; thus he may be said to "starve upon quarrels." How much more would it redound to a man's honour could it be said he had spent four thousand pounds in promoting peace

among men! The amiable behaviour of Edward the
Black Prince, to his prisoner, John, King of France;
the stranger, who generously returned the fortune to
the son, of which the father had deprived him, and
wantonly made the stranger heir of all; the merchant
of Birmingham, who rebuilt a parish church without
telling the world; the four noblemen, who offered their
own heads to save that of their master and friend,
Charles the First; and the poor Presbyterian parson,
who, from choice, sold up all he had to pay his father's
debts, while he starved upon 30*l.* a year, fall short of
this shining character. If one man had been found of
such a description he would have saved Sodom.

A surgeon, who assisted others to live, while he
could hardly live himself, brought a long string of
causes to the Court; among others, he charged Wootton
half a guinea for delivering his wife. Wootton exulted
that the wife was delivered before his arrival, consequently the work was finished to his hands, and as
nothing was done nothing could be required.

Court: Whatever a man *sells*, we have no right to
expect him to *give*; one might beg a draught of ale with
a better grace, at any house, than an alehouse. The
gentlemen of the faculty have three things to dispose of
—their judgment, their time, and their medicines;
whenever they part with any of these they have a right
to payment. We sometimes solicit a reduction of their
demand, not because we think it enormous, but out of
compassion to the needy, and, to their honour, we never
solicited in vain; but we always allow the debt. If
there was not at least a chance of being paid, the poor
might want assistance in the time of distress; a greater
evil than a suit in this Court. We pay the doctor,
whether he cures the complaint, or confirms it; we pay

him for sending us *out* of the world, as well as for bringing us in.—As the surgeon's time was spent in the service of Wootton, he must be rewarded for that time.

XXI.

THE RECKONING.

THE weakness and folly of man is productive of evil; that evil finds a remedy. If the child is disobedient, the vile corrosive called a rod is to reduce him to order. One person attempts to correct the errors of another, who was never able to correct his own. If the imprudent journeyman squanders his whole week's wages in one day he will find his punishment, and his remedy, in starving the other six. The meek husband is goaded into action by the pointed spirit of his wife. There is a remedy, though not always a cure, for every defect, from the gentle rebuke to the halter. The remedy for large debts is the intricate windings of the law; and for small, the Court of Requests, which might easily cure both.

There are particular classes of suitors, besides the quarrelsome, whose faces are repeatedly seen in this Court, as the huckster, the club members, the milkmaid, the publican, &c. These being often wounded, apply often for a cure.

The manufactures of Birmingham are conducted by an amazing number of the lower ranks, a people who are always upon the verge of want without fearing it. The majority of these useful persons keep one main point in view, and to this every consideration gives

way—*how they shall procure a supply of ale.* This
seems the height of their wishes. They are not
votaries of Bacchus, who presides over the wine cask,
but they worship his deputy, who presides over the
ale-barrel.

Thus circumstanced, it is no wonder an *outward*
intimacy arises between the publican and the journeyman. The first endeavours to draw the other to his
house, who is easily drawn, and he in return
endeavours to bilk him. The publican can scarcely
receive much of the other's property without losing his
own. There is not a petty alehouse in the whole town
but chalks up plenty of scores against the journeyman;
there is not one journeyman who strives to diminish,
but to augment them. He is never frightened, like
Belshazzar, at the handwriting on the wall. If he pays
off two, it is with a view to put on three. While he
uses the house the scores rest in peace; when he quits
it he is brought to the Court of Requests. An account
may be carried on between them for years, but the
Court must at last strike the balance. The little
publican lives by his enemies, for he subsists upon
those who are ever ready to bite him.

Marshall was brought before the Court for fifteen
shillings; he acknowledged three shillings and nine-
pence, which he was willing to pay. It appeared that
four people, of whom he was one, had spent an evening, and the above sum, at a public-house, had not
paid their reckoning, and the landlord sued Marshall
for the whole.

Marshall urged, " as he had not drank the whole,
he had no right to pay for the whole; he was but a
fourth of the number, had drank but a fourth of the
drink, and ought to pay but a fourth of the money. No

man had a right to pay for more than he received. The landlord ought to look to each man for his share, and not the whole from one; and that there could be no justice in obliging one man to pay for another."

Court [*to Marshall*] : When a company drink at a public-house they can be considered by the landlord but as one person; they have joined themselves together, and he has no right to put them asunder. He cannot say to one, as he enters, "You may drink," and to another, "You shall not," nor ask any one whether he has money to pay his reckoning. One may treat another, for what he knows, or he may treat the whole. It is a partnership for that night, and what right has the landlord to enquire who finds the capital? They are equally accountable to him for the whole debt. It is not enough that one pays his part, he must take care that the whole is paid; this is *his* concern, not the landlord's. When the partnership dissolves, whether it be at *midday* or *midnight*, every partner is responsible for the debts contracted in the partnership. He that sits silent in company has the same right to pay for the tankard as he who called for it; he who watches at the gate is just as culpable as he who robs the house. If one of them breaks a glass, it is nothing to the landlord who broke it, he can charge it to the company, as well as its contents, and they must settle the matter with the individual. If this was not the case a landlord would soon have his cellar emptied, and nothing left to fill it. One man *with* money might bring a dozen without, who being strangers, the landlord is deprived of his property and his remedy; and as no evil can be brought upon a man, without its attendant cure, for they follow each other like the substance and the shadow, we must charge the debt upon you. He can take any of the company, and that which he takes may demand their shares from the rest. It is to your honour that he singles you out; he thinks you the Pam of the pack.

XXII.

A QUARTER TOO LATE.

How often have I told my dear reader that a member of a sick club sued the stewards for his weekly pay? Yet not so often by five hundred times as I have seen such a cause pass the Bench. There is always a sameness in the name, often in the circumstances, but sometimes they widely differ. Every incident, in some cases, is so much in favour of one side, that we wonder at the stupidity of the other, for suffering it to appear in public; he brings the laugh of the crowd upon himself; every eye can see the folly but his own. In other cases a decision depends upon a combination of circumstances; but a third, like a spider at the extremity of a slender thread, is directed by the smallest breath.

When a sick member wishes to cling to the box, and the well members to shake him off, and shun him as an infected person, it is no other than a declaration of war between the parties; the cause requires a minute investigation, and at last turns upon a delicate point.

A member of a sick-club declared himself upon the box. The club, wishing to rid themselves of an expensive brother, declared " he had forfeited his right by being disguised in liquor; by being seen gambling, employed at his calling, and what was worst of all, he

pretended to be lame of an arm, yet they had seen him
with that very arm lift the tankard to his mouth.   Any
one crime in this long catalogue was sufficient to
disinherit him."

The Court observed that these heavy charges were
rather *asserted* than *proved*; that they could not act
against a sick member upon hearsay evidence, and
asked if they could substantiate their allegations; this
not being done, they were going to decide for the sick,
when it appeared that a member lost his right by omit-
ting his payments for six club-nights; that our member
had omitted five, and finding himself sick had, on the
sixth, taken one night's pay to keep the road to the
box open.   But though he spent his evening with the
members, he forgot to tender the money till the club
hours were expired, and his right fell by that small
neglect.

Though this trifling omission would have been
excused in any other member, and in him at any other
time, yet the Court conceived they were obliged to
dismiss the cause in favour of the club, for though they
had a right to break their own laws by granting a
favour, the Court had not; and the neglect of a quarter
of an hour was as much a breach of the contract as a
quarter of a year.

XXIII.

THE BASTARD.

A TRIFLE may preserve a man's character; a trifle may lose it. The world can only judge by what they see; as every man has two sides, it is prudent only to exhibit the bright. Not more than half our conduct, situations, and characters will bear the public eye; the rest is hid. Our very race is preserved in secret; a man would be ashamed to be found by another where he is often obliged to find himself. It was monstrously provoking when Miss Jenny was accidentally seen without her headdress; she cannot appear till she has brushed into her cheeks the virgin blush, and bitten her lips into scarlet. Every one has concerns he wishes to hide; if he does not, the world to which he divulges them will brand him for a fool. B— G— asked John W——n if it was a crime to be connected with a girl? "Yes, if it becomes public." An old Grecian said, "that not only his actions, but even his thoughts, were so pure that he wished there were windows in his breast that the world might see them in their simplicity"; but if my late friend Henry Henn, Esq., had heard this declaration of pride and ignorance he would have said to the standers-by, "Take care of your pockets."

One would think a character but little regarded by the owner who voluntarily fools it away for six shillings. He may be said to value it as the cock in Æsop valued the diamond, which he gave up for a grain of barley. He may lose it for that sum, but not regain it.

There is a degree of sameness in the actions of
men, but their prudence consists in conducting them;
one enjoys a fair character who does not deserve it,
another deserves a better than he possesses.

A defendant was sued by a woman for a debt of
six shillings. He thought it unjust, but would submit
to the judgment of the Bench. A girl being pregnant
by him, he agreed with the plaintiff " that the girl for
privacy, should lie in at her house, she should nurse
her, and find all necessary diet, during the month, for
twenty-four shillings, but if the girl went to work before
the time expired a proportionate sum should be
deducted."   At the end of three weeks the girl applying
herself to labour, the defendant from thence concluded
he had no right to pay for the fourth week, though the
plaintiff had supported her and the child upon his own
agreement.

Court: If the girl and her child lay upon the plaintiff
a month she ought to be paid for a month; this seems
to have been the meaning of both. The only point to
be determined is, whether you or the girl ought to pay.
A bargain was made with you, but none with her. A
woman has been known to enter upon business at the
end of one week, and if this had been the case, ought
she to have maintained her four?   You must settle
with the girl for the profit of her work during the fourth
week, or it may go towards the next lying-in, but you
must be responsible for this. If you trick the plaintiff
in your first distress, you may chance to want a friend
in your second. You have now sported a character of
value against a trifle, and lost both. Another would
wish to hide what you have made public. Fame, with
her hundred tongues, can carry our defects into the
world without our assistance.

XXIV.

"THE TEMPEST," AS IT WAS ACTED BY THEIR MAJESTIES' SERVANTS AT THE THEATRE IN BIRMINGHAM.

IN all partnerships, or connections which are successful, it is easy for the partners to agree. Prosperity raises the smile. But when matters run retrograde the fault is laid upon every back, but none can be found that will bear it. When G. and L. became bankrupts, "You see," says G. to a creditor, "what you suffer by the conduct of your friend L." The same creditor afterwards saw L. "You see," says L., "what you suffer by the conduct of your friend G."

The trades in Birmingham everlastingly fluctuate; the emoluments and the fashions have changed so often that one would think nothing new could offer. Yet these changes are infinite. Change is invention; invention is the life of trade. But I know no trade in Birmingham that has undergone so many vicissitudes as the stage. The scenes first opened in the apartments of a horse, such as the shed, the hovel, and the stable; and the performer, like the inhabitant, regaled on something like bran for his meat, and water for his drink. But the comedian, sailing along the tide of fourscore years, sometimes moving two leagues forward and sometimes one backward, now figures in an elegant style. He appears in character, acts with propriety, and is the gentleman off the stage as well as on. Many causes contributed to his success, as the increase of commerce, which has produced an increase

of wealth, of pleasure, and of taste : these tend to
encourage merit.   The stage, which scarcely furnished
water-gruel for its heroes, now draws 300*l.* a week
from Birmingham. The town is treated with characters
that please, and pays willingly for the treat.   But in
one of these backsliding intervals which happened
about 1773, the credit and the profit of the stage were
at a low ebb; instead of drawing three hundred they
could not draw three score. The receipts did not pay
the expense, and every party was dissatisfied. The
town upbraided the manager, because he offered them
bad performers; and the manager upbraided the town,
because they would not pay for good.   Ill-success
produced quarrels among the comedians themselves,
every one had blame laid upon him, and always threw
it upon another. The house was sometimes so thin
that the few who attended had their money returned,
and all departed in peace, but the actors.

Though the manager had hired his Majesties'
Servants at a weekly stipend, yet he concluded, as they
did not perform, they had no right to receive pay; if
he was no gainer by them, why should they be gainers
by him? He withheld their wages. But though his
Majesties' Servants had been used to change like the
chameleon, yet as they had not, like him, been used to
live upon air, they resolved that one of them should
try the fate of his cause in the Court of Requests, as
upon this determination would depend the others.
—Wrighten sued the manager for 1*l.* 11*s.* 6*d.*, one
week's salary.

The manager alleged it was an ancient maxim,
" Where nothing is done, nothing can be demanded ";
that it would be unreasonable to maintain a body of
people without some profit arising from that body to

maintain himself; that the loss was too great for *one* to bear, each therefore ought to bear a part; that he subsisted by their performance, and if they did not perform he could not subsist; how then could he pay?

It was remarked in reply that the parties were bound by an agreement, upon the strength of which the comedians had entered his service. He could demand their attendance, and they his money; had they denied assistance, at proper seasons, the fault had been theirs, and the demand ceased; he must find them employment, and they must find attendance; that they could not be accountable for thin houses; that the servant had nothing to do with the profit of the master. They were, like other servants, upon a certainty; profit and loss must rest with the manager, as with other masters. If the emoluments had arisen beyond expectation, would the manager have conferred those emoluments upon them, or could they have demanded them? If the profits cannot be claimed by the actor, it follows the loss cannot be fixed upon him.

The manager, convinced by these reasons, cheerfully acquiesced in a decision against himself, and departed the Court with a complaisant smile.

XXV.

THE FEMALE CONTEST.

THE habit of our mind is so various that at one time we would not divulge a secret, even to a friend in private, for seven guineas, while at another we should publicly proclaim it to the world for seven shillings; thus a man may forfeit his life by robbing another of a

few pence who could not be persuaded to part with
that life even for ten thousand pounds. This is the
animal of reason!

Cooper sued Anson for " seven shillings, of good
and lawful money of Great Britain, for goods sold
and delivered," by one wife to the other. Both the
husbands were of still character, and though their
names stood in the front of the cause, they did not
appear, had nothing to do with the trial, which was
wholly conducted by their wives.

Anson's wife acquiesced in the justice of the debt,
but remarked that Cooper himself had been familiar
with her, that she had frequently granted him all the
favours she could grant, and that a close connection
like this cancelled every demand.

Coop.: When my husband was concerned with her,
I make no doubt he answered every claim she made
upon him, he never solicits favours without pay; the
connection and the debt are different things. It rested
with her to make a bargain.

Court: When you settled accounts with the husband, was this debt mentioned?

A.: No!

Coop.: I think it very hard she should take away
both my husband and my money [*with a smile*].

A.: If I gave him all I could, I have a right, in
return, to all I owed, or I am ill used.

Coop.: It is I that am ill used, and have a right
to complain.

A.: She should keep her husband at home.

C.: Perhaps you will not permit her.

Coop.: I love my husband. He minds the main
chance; his only fault is going after the girls, and,
as I cannot prevent it, I excuse it.

C. : Why, you shew more philosophy than half your own sex, and the whole of ours; you give your bread to the hungry, and fast yourself.

A. : I will never pay the debt.

Coop. : Then I will have an execution.

C. : It would be a pity to send the husband to prison, because the wife goes astray. You add one affliction to another; besides this would give the delinquents a fairer opportunity.

Coop. : I only want my money. I do not complain at their intercourse, for if he has not her he will have another, and I had rather be at variance with one woman than a troop.

C. : If we judge from personal accomplishments, the odds are much in your favour.

Coop. : Variety is not in one, a truth she is well convinced of.

C. : The plaintiff shews an amiable temper in pardoning an evil she cannot cure, a temper seldom found in the sex, but is worthy of cultivation: it carries its own reward. The likeliest way to reclaim is to forgive. The defendant, too, takes the best method for her own cure. No man who has a character at stake will venture it with a woman who is the trumpeter of her own crimes, an instance rarely met with. By accusing herself, she accuses him. If a woman cannot hide her conduct, modesty forbids her to tell it; she leaves that for another. This woman may fairly be said to govern, with an absolute sway, every animal with antlers in her dominions, or she durst not have divulged so important a secret. There is no danger of a prosecution, for the husband is not allowed to proceed without orders from the guilty wife. Every tender feeling is abolished, or she would not court the hisses of the crowd.

If a man enters the precincts of his neighbour, redress is not with us. Debts only are cognisable in this Court. That the claim before us is just is not doubted, that it has not been cancelled is allowed by both; we must therefore make an order for payment; but, out of tenderness to an injured husband, we shall make those payments easy.

XXVI.

THE HUNDRED-TONGUE CLUB.

ALL social communities are conducted by wisdom, or they are ill conducted. With her aid they stand; without it they fall. Ability introduces method, method perseverance, and perseverance success. A single capacity may, with ease to itself, accomplish mighty things; nay, there are but few undertakings too great for one man to achieve. Guided by wisdom, Marlborough conquered, Brindley planned, and Pitt governed. Voltaire says, " the man who is able to conduct a family is able to conduct a kingdom." The same talents which aid the master, in the choice of his servants, will the prince in that of his ministers. If one can lead his children, the other can lead his people. But though the powers in both are the same, there is not one man in ten able to conduct either. It is impossible for perfection and human nature to exist together, and yet in my narrow circle of acquaintance I could point out two or three of amazing judgment, who upon every question seem to think right.

If I mention a society, composed of many people, without a leader, every one speaking at the same time, and striving who shall speak loudest; not one knowing how to write their name, scarcely to sign a cross, or with which hand to sign it; it may fairly be supposed I am introducing a *female club.*

We abound with clubs of the feminine gender; some composed of young girls, some of wives, or widows, and some a mixture of all. A mantua-maker, to introduce business, will establish a *gown club.* The members subscribe weekly, and ballot for their chance. A *stays club* is brought forward by the stay-maker, but both he and the mantua-maker are fortunate if they recover payment. A woman may be rigged from head to foot by a female club, provided the expense shall not exceed a certain amount. I have not yet heard of an institution, which would bear the name of the *husband club*, where a girl might ballot herself into matrimony for a weekly sum. Such a society would not be limited to a small number; a member would not lose her chance for non-attendance, nor, till married, be brought to the Court of Conscience for non-payment. No club would be so closely followed. The one solitary club-night a week would increase to seven. Of all institutions this would be the most acceptable, notwithstanding some of the lower class among us know already how to erect themselves into wives at sixteen.

A woman sued the stewardess of a sick-club for eight shillings, two weeks' pay. About twelve of the members appeared to oppose her. The case being extremely plain, and the Commissioners being masters of it in a few seconds, they left this body of active females to the exercise of their favourite powers, the

6

powers of eloquence. Every tongue had its full scope for some minutes, while a silent smile sat upon the Bench. If you have seen a group of pedlars quarrelling for a stall at a fair, you have a tolerable idea of our present contest. This confusion of tongues would well bear the name of Babel revived. As words were plentiful, and ideas scarce, the same sounds were continually repeated, like the chimes in a steeple, but loud as the peal. The Commissioners could see, what is seldom seen, twelve females without disguise; and their passions take their natural turn without control. They could observe how the violent use of the tongue promoted a friction in the fluids, the friction produced a warmth, the warmth kindled into a fire, the fire began to redden in the cheek, and sparkle in the eye, when, to prevent the rising flames, the Court remarked—

By a certificate from a gentleman of the faculty she has been ill three weeks, which is corroborated by her face, and allowed by you. She is a stranger to us, but she carries the air of prudence, and, if we can judge from appearances, we should think her more inclined to subsist by her own labour than by yours. You allege she has forfeited her right by breaking the articles, in being found at work; but that work appears to be no more than assisting another to cook a small joint for her family dinner, which a woman is able to do even in extreme sickness. The discovery was much to her credit. You strain the words beyond what they can bear; you might as well exclude a sick woman for pinning her hat, or buckling her shoe. The plain meaning of the clause is, " if she labours for a livelihood, she shall be expelled." We shall act by her, as every one of you would wish us, in her situation, to act by you, make an order in her favour. We do not

advise a restraint of the tongue, that would be advising
the fierce north-east wind to blow softer, but we advise
you to remember an expression dropped by the first
of men, " Behave to others as you wish them to behave
to you."

XXVII.

CHARACTER.

THERE is scarcely a word in the English language
more perverted than that of *riches*.   We limit the sense
to money, or what money will purchase.   But riches,
like the various coins which usually compose them,
appear in a multitude of forms, and all, like the coins,
are extremely acceptable.   Whatever is valuable
property, not possessed by others, is riches.

Very few things are worth more to a man than his
limbs, and yet he who commands two hands is not
rich, because most men hold as many.   But he who
unfortunately has but one may be reckoned poor,
because he is below the medium.   A head is of no
particular value, because every man has one, but there
may be some difference in the lining.   As every head
is not fraught with wisdom, knowledge, wit, or good
sense, those who are have a property beyond the
generality of men, and may be counted rich.   They
who are not holders of these treasures, do not much
value them, because they are unknown; they who are,
esteem them above the price of purchase.

Health is riches; he who keeps it, keeps a jewel of
inestimable worth.

Another species of valuable property is *youth*.
The young experience variety of pleasures from which

age is cut off. Like the bee, they can draw sweetness without poison. They seem made for the world, and the world for them. Youth commands pleasure, and pleasure is a fortune which the man of threescore has spent, never to be recovered. If two men in the commercial line possess 10,000*l*. each, one aged thirty, the other sixty, the man of thirty is twice as rich as the other, for he can easily double his fortune while he doubles his years. Time is equivalent to money.

Beauty is a gem of the first water; those who do not own it, affect to despise it; those who do, think it invaluable. It often covers defects, and sometimes makes up the loss of all. Miss Fanny B. would rather kill with her beauty, than part with it for money. All feel it, admire it, wish it. Those who possess it assume more airs of pride than those who possess money, which proves its superior value.

Whoever possesses a *character* is master of true wealth. He need not court, he will be courted. We have the authority of Solomon, who was read in man, "that a good name is preferable to riches." Perhaps this property is, of all others, the most durable; for riches may make themselves wings and fly away, talents may fail, health decline, youth wear off, and beauty fade, while a fair character may continue for life. This is the only property a man has an absolute power over, all the others may be taken from him, but if he loses this it must be by his own consent; he may discard honesty, but it will never discard him. It is a feast on which he may ever regale. He, like his great grandfather Adam, solaces in the paradise of innocence, and an angel will rather protect him within than drive him out.

Taylor sued S. for one pound eight shillings, which being denied, the Court entered into the merits of the claim. It appeared that Taylor worked as a wheelwright many weeks for S., who at several times made payments in small and irregular sums. Taylor exhibited as fair an account as could be expected from a man more used to the axe than the pen, and the tankard than either. S.'s account consisted more in words than writing.

Court: The vouchers produced by both throw some light upon the subject, but our perfect knowledge of your characters throws more. When Taylor is sober he is civil, well-behaved, industrious, and well understands his business, perhaps too well for fourteenpence a day, the price he charges. When he is drunk, which is as often as he can, he is a perfect noodle, but in both cases strictly honest. He never injures any man but himself. His weakness tempts others to injure *him*. Two requisites constitute a rogue—inclination and ability; he holds neither. When the character stands firm, it will support the man.

A different glass must be held up to view the character of S. Dark, shrewd, contemplative, he, like Cassius, *designs* with caution before he executes. He possesses two requisites, at least, more than his antagonist. The strong in every species overpower the weak. An account may be ravelled with design, that profit, as in cases of fire and tumult, may be drawn from confusion. While the simple reposes in his own innocence, he may be caught in the wiles of the crafty. From the accounts exhibited, and the characters which exhibit them, we may safely pronounce for Taylor.

XXVIII.

THE NAME UNKNOWN.

I SHALL introduce the following case with a proverb, a story, a metaphor, and two remarks; and close it with releasing its stubborn hero from the prison.

" He who digs a pit for another may perchance fall into it himself."

The story of Mordecai and Haman is exactly in point, but I shall waive it for another less known. When Edward VI. had suppressed an insurrection in Cornwall, Kingston, a provost, was sent with dreadful powers to Bodmin, and waiting on the mayor, told him he wished to have a gallows erected, for there must be an execution in town after dinner. The mayor gave the necessary orders, fixed his eye upon a neighbouring miller, whom he knew had been concerned in the revolt, invited the provost to his house, where they dined, and drank together as friends. After dinner, the mayor, impatient of delay, told the provost he had punctually executed his orders. " You will oblige me," says the provost, " if you will lead me to the place "; which done, " Is it strong enough?" says the officer; " Doubtless," says the magistrate. " Then get up and try," says the provost. " You are not in earnest!" says the other. " Indeed I am," replied the provost, " for you are one of the rebels, and the gallows you erected for another is only for yourself," and immediately executed him.

Innocence is the surest guard. A man may fence himself round with thorns to prevent the approach of an enemy, but, if attacked, that very fence may prevent his retreat, and the thorns wound him.

An ingenuous conduct will be more useful to a man, even in the day of distress, than subterfuge. Equivocations operate against himself.

John Flint was sued for 1*l*. 15s. He applied to a Commissioner, and alleged the name was wrong. " This is not a proper place," replied the Commissioner, " to make an objection; you may plead the misnomer in Court, where it will be attended to." At the trial he made the same plea, when the Bench, of course, asked his name.

Flint: I will not tell you.

Court: We have a right to know your real name, or we must proceed against you in this.

F.: I am not ashamed of my name.

C.: You are backward in owning it. Are you the man who owes the money?

F.: Yes.

C.: If you declare your name, we shall treat you with all the lenity your case deserves; if not, we will enter an order for immediate payment, in which case you will be sent to prison.

F.: I will declare it when I please.

C.: We have given the defendant every chance to prevent mischief to himself. He seeks another's destruction, but finds his own. The snare has caught him which he laid for the plaintiff. If a plea like this was admitted it would totally end all proceedings; a man need only allege his name is wrong, and justice dwindles into a shadow.

The Court made the order accordingly, and instantly committed him. He threatened for an hour, then mourned for many. Repentance excites pity. The Court, touched with compassion, wished to release him, but were unable to revoke their orders. From repeated

applications they at length prevailed with the plaintiff
to take his security for the debt and costs.

XXIX.

THE FEMALE NOTE.

RIGHT and wrong are divided by a most delicate
and crooked line. By its slenderness, it cannot be
easily seen; by its crookedness, the premises of one
seem to verge upon the other.

L. sued Hunt, for which debt he produced a note
of hand; Hunt declared he never gave one. Upon
examination the note proved to be signed and given
by Hunt's wife.

Court [*to L.*] : The debt may be just, and we believe
it is, for we are too well acquainted with your probity
to doubt it; but you cannot recover by this note. The
giver has no power to give. The debt may stand
without it, but not with it. It appears by this note
how difficult it is to keep that active thing called a wife
within compass. But few women know their sphere,
and but few men dare teach them; the full liberty of
a female pen is dangerous. Though the laws allow
our wives but a narrow latitude, yet the dear creatures
know well how to wind round our hearts, to direct our
persons, influence our conduct, and induce us to act
under their direction. But if they were allowed to act
of themselves, they might quickly sign away a fortune.
The haberdasher and the china shop would divide the
profits of the week; their notes would be negotiated
through the hands of milliners and mantua-makers,
till there would be *no effects*, and the notes would, like

this, be returned, with a protest for non-payment. The use of the *tongue* is the province of a woman, not the pen; the first is a bubble, which begins and ends in air, let it alone, and it hurts nothing; but the pen, like the black, cloven, lower end of Satan, were it not prevented by power, might deal out destruction without mercy. Our love for the sweet little dears will oblige us to set bounds to their conduct; we honour them, though we cannot honour their notes.

XXX.

THE WIDOWED WIFE.

Perhaps we may safely adopt this plain maxim, If a man parts with his property upon the credit of another, he ought to have it returned, if it can be effected by any reasonable means. If this is allowed, it follows that if the debtor has consumed the property trusted to his honour, his future time, his effects, and his abilities, in a moderate degree, ought to be responsible to the creditor. A man having spent all is no acquittance. He who does mischief, ought to make reparation.

I have delivered the sentiments of the Court upon the two foregoing examples; the third is that of a wife, whose husband has left her. We abound with instances of this kind, some with children, some without. There is nothing she can call her own, but the arts of labour and imprudence. If the first of these will not supply the second, and it seldom will, the defect is made up by the labour of others. Every species of finesse is practised to overreach those who trade in the necessaries of life. She subsists by a little ready money, and a little credit. The money is temporary, the credit eternal. Her depredations are chalked upon every huxter's door in the neighbourhood; nor will she leave a shop while the master continues to chalk on; but the moment he desists, she sets him at defiance with an absent husband, and beats the bushes for fresh game.

Can it be sound policy in a government to shelter a person under the wing of the law, who designs to plunder? The husband has been gone many years, perhaps into another part of the kingdom, into Ireland, or the king's service; neither is it certain she has one; she has contracted the debt; how must it be paid? It is said every evil has its remedy, where then is the remedy for this? Why may not this widowed wife be considered as a single woman? It appears more agreeable to justice, as the husband is out of the question, to make her responsible for the debt who contracted it; nay, there seems a kind of injustice in charging the husband with an act in which he had no concern. There is a material difference between obliging a wife to pay her husband's debts, and her own.

A person was sued for 1*l.* 6*s.* in the name of Susanna Bower; it appeared her husband had been gone to sea some years, that she had since lived gaily with the money earned by the family, and that arising from the contribution under which she had the address to lay the huxters. She was well acquainted with the various methods of getting the effects of others into her hands, but not of returning them.

Court: Causes like this frequently come before us; we behold them with concern, for the delinquent retreats triumphant. The laws of England consider the husband accountable for the debts of the wife; though she is the sole actress, they do not suppose her to act. She enjoys unmolested the fruits of another's labour. The plaintiff is wronged without a remedy. Common justice directs that she who has done the wrong should make reparation. If she has no effects to accomplish this, her future talents, as in other cases, ought to be employed for that purpose. As this Court is detached from the law, we apprehend no evil could arise from a judgment against her; but as the Courts above have not given us a precedent, we shall not venture to set the example. We must, therefore, with regret, dismiss the cause, suffer the offender to escape unpunished, and the innocent plaintiff to be defrauded according to law.

XXXI.

THE BENCH STORMED.

THE man who acts in a public capacity, holds himself up to public view. His actions are scrutinised, and though he proceeds according to the best of his powers, is often condemned. To *act* is to displease. Posterity will do him the justice he deserves, for they never err, but his contemporaries " see through a glass darkly "; the hand of prejudice presents to the jaundiced eye a false medium. What character has been more traduced than Lord Mansfield's? What character has less deserved it? Before a man steps into a public walk, he may " sit down," and ask himself this question, or if he stands, it makes no great difference, Can I be contented to do good, and be evil spoken of?

If he cannot, he had better rest in a private station; if he can, let his labour be that of rectitude, and let him trust to the next generation for his reward.

I have known a cause very near taking a wrong bias by mere bully, " the voice of words " has stifled that of justice. The Commissioner who suffers himself to be guided by sound, without argument, displays a weakness unbecoming the Bench. Every evidence has been in favour of him who had not the gift of speaking, while vehemence without right has borne down the man, and influenced the Court.

A tenant in arrears to his landlord, who was a Quaker, persuaded his father, and that father's friend, to give their joint note for 1l. 12s. to prevent a distress; this appeased the Quaker till more rent became due. The father afterwards sent 1l. 11s. 6d. to the Quaker. The Quaker sued the friend for the 1l. 12s.

The question to be considered by the Court was simply this, whether the Quaker was obliged to appropriate the guinea and a half towards the note, or had liberty to charge it for subsequent rent?

The friend, who was a butcher, offered many words, without one reason; he treated his antagonist with as little ceremony, when in Court, and the Commissioners themselves, when out, as the cattle he slaughtered: " they must have a feeling in the money-box, or they could never determine against him. They could not understand the case, neither would they hear it."

Happy is that Commissioner, who, upon the review of a determination, sees no reason to repent it, but while the storm thunders round his ears, can take peaceable shelter in his own breast, and smile at the tempest.

Many accusations lie against the Bench; the chief is, that as one of the parties only can win, the other supposes himself ill-treated, therefore accusation will lie against them till they can find a way to satisfy both; another is, *they will not hear the loser*, but does it follow they are bound to hear from him the same sounds continually repeated like the horrid midnight notes of a pair of cats making love. I never knew an instance where the Commissioners finished a cause while the parties had anything to offer; but perhaps they are justified for putting an end to the contest, when the complainant, for want of new matter, repeats the same thing twice over.

The butcher, fond of speaking himself, would not suffer another; the Court, therefore, could only remark in broken sentences. That no mention being made, for what use the money should be appropriated, left the Quaker at liberty; that if the money was meant to discharge the note, why was not the note demanded? that the sum sent, was not the sum mentioned in the security, therefore could not be considered an equivalent; that the note was given because the tenant owed the money, and as he still owed it, why should the note be cancelled? If the tenant had ever been out of the Quaker's debt, the note would have been invalid, though not taken up, for it ought not to have its strength renewed by a second debt, without a second contract; but as it was given because money was due, and that money remained due, they could have no pretence to destroy it: for these reasons they considered themselves bound to decide for the Quaker; and the butcher will recover from the tenant. The decision left the butcher in a flame, the father and mother breathing a spirit of revenge, and the Commissioners never to be forgiven.

XXXII.

THE COAT AND MANY OWNERS.

PEMBERTON was a stranger, of a moderate capacity, about fifty, had married a girl of twenty, who appeared handsome, modest, and agreeable, but not much wiser than her husband. She had never seen the world, and he was never able to see it. This loving couple, with one child, in 1786, came to seek their fortunes in Birmingham, and took up their abode in Moor Street, in a den of thieves. The husband was easily enticed to get drunk, and treat the whole crew, which expense, with three shillings borrowed by Hill, broke him. Hill then persuaded him out of his coat, which he gave to A, and he pawned it to B. C fetched it out of pawn, and sold it to D for two shillings and twopence. D having mended it, sold it to E for four shillings, and perhaps this hackneyed coat, in a fortnight more, would have travelled through the whole alphabet. Pemberton sued Hill for thirteen shillings and sixpence, half a guinea the coat, and three shillings borrowed.

Money is the grand standard to which all property is brought to find its value; this is the only certainty we know; and except property of every kind has been tried by this standard, it cannot be pronounced a debt, nor recovered in this Court. If Pemberton has a right to charge his coat at half a guinea, why not at half a score? If the bounds of value are not exactly prescribed, those bounds, like space, become infinite. Had Pemberton been defrauded of his coat while new, it would have borne a certain price, but becoming second-hand, that certainty ceases; the Bench cannot treat it as a debt.

All the parties appeared; some of them I knew had practised the arts of deception for thirty years. They spoke loud in favour of themselves, as people usually do whose actions will not speak for them. They alleged against Pemberton that he was a *foreigner* and a *Papist*.

Court: As he who wilfully sets the house in a flame is the first to cry out fire, so he who *injures* is the first to censure the injured. Pemberton being a stranger, should have taught you another conduct. A stranger is entitled to our civility and protection, but you consider him an object of plunder. You also accuse him of being a Roman Catholic; this proves nothing against *his* religion, but much against your own, for it proves a Protestant is both able and willing to rob a Papist.

We direct that E. shall relinquish his four shilling bargain to D. and that D. shall return the coat to Pemberton, paying her three shillings—two shillings and twopence for the purchase, and tenpence for mending, which, being paid on Hill's account, brings the coat to the standard of value, and adds three shillings to his debt; we shall therefore make an order against him for six, and recommend a lesson, he will never learn, to shew kindness to strangers, and justice to all.

XXXIII.

THE CLOUD OF WITNESSES.

EVIDENCES, like snuffers, were intended to improve the light, but like them, they often extinguish it. Cut short by the bungling hand, and hid in darkness, neither the cause, nor the candle, can readily be lighted again. If only two antagonists oppose each other, the dim subject is confined to a narrow compass, which the Commissioner can better inspect; but if each adds his man the case becomes more complex, and by multiplying evidence, confusion is multiplied. A dozen of ale is able to produce a dozen of voices; each follows his principal, and totally obliterates intelligence. Instead of the Commissioner being assisted by the light which others can throw upon the subject, he is obliged to extinguish their light, and follow his own.

Hill drove a hackney coach, and kept, or rather starved, a pair of horses. He declared he had taken a stable of Mills, at one shilling a week; that Mills was to find straw for his horses, in consideration of the manure they made; that he being in arrears for rent, and Mills for straw, he had purchased as much as cost him twenty-five shillings, which he expected to set off in the rent, when they reckoned; but Mills taking a distress, and recovering the rent, he now sued him for the twenty-five shillings advanced for straw.

This smooth tale was flatly contradicted by Mills. After the two chiefs had maintained the conflict with equal bravery, each drew up his battalion of evidences, which supported the contest with fury, but victory declared for neither. The Bench could plainly perceive that when the parties engaged had exhausted their ammunition, each had his corps of reserve, ready to march up to renew the attack. They could also perceive that after three long examinations the cause ravelled upon their hands.

Court: We are got into a wilderness barricaded with evidences; every one of them knows a way out, and would willingly lead us, but the farther we proceed the more difficult the road; we will retreat to the ground from whence we departed. Nothing has been proved but contradictions. We dare not administer oaths, they are too sacred to be trifled with; both sides would willingly take them, for he who publicly *asserts* will publicly *swear*. But as neither their words, nor their oaths, elucidate the case, we shall set aside both, leave them to enjoy their purchase-pot, and proceed upon our own judgment.

That the stable was taken at a shilling a week is allowed by both, consequently Mills had a right to his distress. The whole weight of the matter consists in the bargain for straw. If we attend to the present scarcity of that article, we cannot suppose such a contract to exist, because the straw would be four times the value of the manure. If we further consider the hungry state of the poor horses, and that Mills must find straw for the inside of the belly, as well as the out, a thought that could not escape him, we must suppose him, before he could ratify such a bargain, weak enough to give ten shillings for one. Our decision, therefore, will rest upon this short question: as Mills furnished some straw, and received some manure, how much was he benefited by this exchange of property?

7

Both parties being taken by surprise, were unpre-
pared for an answer to this simple question; it was
treated as comprehending mysteries never meant; all
were willing to misunderstand it; the fear of being
caught brought out replies foreign or evasive, and this
little question, "being compassed about by so great
a cloud of witnesses," was with great difficulty preserved by the Bench from being lost in obscurity.
From the best intelligence they could obtain, the
difference might be about five shillings, which was
ordered in favour of Hill.

XXXIV.

A CLUB CONDUCTED WITHOUT A MAN.

If we see a bargain made between two heads, and
we may see five hundred every day, we may safely
conclude it originates from self-interest; this is the
enlivening principle which warms into action; the
hinge upon which we turn—the pole to which we
point.　This motive influences every man, from
Richard Duke of York, who bargained for a kingdom,
to John Byard, who sells a farthing club.　But when
we see an *absurd* bargain, we may easily trace its
pedigree to a weak or a roguish head.　If an extra
advantage lies on one side, inability is sure to lie on
the other.

A tailor, who by the size of his body seemed in
reality but the ninth of a man, and to possess but a
ninth of capacity, found means, through pity, to
assemble a few friends, and erect a clothes club.　They
were to meet weekly, spend twopence, and contribute

a shilling to the box. When the box became ripe for a ballot, the winner might purchase a suit of clothes, of a certain value, where he pleased, but the tailor had a right to claim the making, and charge twelve shillings.

A fortunate member, instead of giving the tailor a *suit* to make, gave him only a coat and breeches, for which he paid him nine shillings, and the tailor brought him to the Court for the other three.

Court: All societies of men, whether they compose a powerful kingdom or a petty club, are governed by their own laws, but laws without punishment can no more be productive than a tree without a root. It is enacted in the case before us that the member shall employ the tailor, but where is the infliction if he does not? This Court has always countenanced social compact, but our decisions are often prevented by their weak or absurd laws; nor can we wonder, for if 558 members, which compose the House of Commons, are not able to guard a law, how can it be expected from the ninth of a man. Had their articles, upon non-compliance, demanded a forfeiture, the road would have been open before us. There are other inducements to dismiss the cause. As the tailor did not do the work, it is not reasonable he should be paid. No debt exists. Again, if we order payment, the member will pay for what he never received; and if, in future, the tailor refuses to work, the member can have no remedy, for the power of the Court will be cut off by a decision; we therefore advise him to furnish the tailor with materials for a waistcoat.

XXXV.

THE STAMP.

THINGS are unfavourably circumstanced when law and equity directly oppose each other, so that one of them must fall. The only question then to be considered is, which must be sacrificed? We should reasonably suppose equity ought to stand upon an everlasting basis.

Should the weary and sleepy traveller retire to the corner of a field for repose, and while he sleeps the farmer cut off his retreat by surrounding him with a hedge of thorns, the law says the farmer has a right to make his hedge where he pleases, and the other, none to destroy it. Is the traveller then to perish because the law must be kept? But if the law will vindicate the farmer in erecting the fence, equity will the traveller in breaking it down. Upon what unfavourable ground then does the Commissioner stand, who both ought and wishes to adhere to the laws of his country, but is obliged to break them? He must either relinquish conscience or law. A point like this, even unconnected with the lawyer, would bear an everlasting dispute, because both sides seem right. The weak and absurd minister who brings him into this situation, by introducing an Act to infringe the powers of equity, ought to be deprived of his political existence, and his works follow him. It is allowed on all hands that the expenses of government must be supplied; but it must also be allowed that the consequences of an act should be seen, and its evils avoided. Because a case is *law*, does it follow it is *right*? When this contrariety appears, it brings with it no alternative : decision must lie in the breast of equity.

A plaintiff possessed a note of hand, not upon stamped paper, given by the defendant for 5*l*. 6*s*. and payable by one shilling a week. Thirty weeks being due, he sued for thirty shillings. An attorney pleaded for the defendant, with an air of decisive triumph, that a note without a stamp could not, by Act of Parliament, be admitted as evidence in any Court. That the note annihilated itself; that the whole debt of 5*l*. 6*s*. might stand without it, and that the plaintiff might sue for 1*l*. 19*s*. 11*d*., which must comprehend the whole.

Court : No law ought to set aside an evidence which can elucidate a fact. If a Judge shuts his eyes against information, he shuts them against justice. Our oath does not oblige us to proceed according to law, but good conscience. A Commissioner must decide as he is convinced. An Act of Parliament cannot convert wrong into right. This note, even without a stamp, convinces our consciences of two things, that a certain sum was agreed between the parties as a debt, and that a shilling a week should be the mode of payment. Neither side can break either of these articles without injustice; then what right has law or we? If we are convinced the agreement is founded in equity, how can we reconcile it to ourselves to destroy it? The note proves both, neither doth any contradiction arise against it, except an act which proves nothing but weakness in the minister, and necessity in the State, Should we destroy the debt, and be asked afterwards, whether we thought it just and the bargain fair? we should answer in the affirmative; should we again be asked why we did not give it the owner? we could find no answer but the blush of a culprit.

The same arguments hold good with regard to receipts, which we may also consider a tax upon justice. Should a man give a receipt without a stamp, and afterwards make a second claim, though we leave pains and penalties to superior Courts, yet, being convinced the debt was paid, the suit would be discharged.

Though it has not been the practice of this Court to divide a debt, except the contract for such division was made in writing, yet why may not a verbal division hold good? If 5l. 6s. is owing by one man to another, and they verbally agree the money shall be paid by instalments, neither of them can justly dissolve the agreement; consequently the stamp is out of the question, they ought to be supported, and the Court to lend their assistance in discharging the debt.

As law cannot bind conscience, and as we remain bound by the oath of rectitude, we must decide for the plaintiff, and express our regret that an Act of the Legislature should clash with equity.

XXXVI.

THE STUMBLING WIFE.

THE intricate windings of the law are deceitful. The traveller pursues a false road, and sees with false lights, till the *ignis fatuus* conducts him to the end of a melancholy journey; when from being a sufferer he finds himself a greater; whereas, had his neighbours been invested with summary powers, they might have

put a period to the contest, perhaps without a lawyer,
but really without a loss to the parties.

The increase of causes in this Court has increased
the attendance of the professors of the law, who, fond
of the mazy track they have long pursued, would
quickly convert it from a Court of Equity to a Court
of Law. Scarcely a day passes without the appearance of a lawyer; who, hired, like a Swiss, in defence
of his employer, boldly encounters his antagonist, but
with this difference of wages—the Swiss fights for
seven shillings a week, the lawyer for seven shillings
a cause. Two consequences attend him as closely as
his client, or his fee, the business will be stagnated,
and the cause disguised. Whenever we behold the
champion enter, we may safely order dinner to wait;
and his manner of opening the case is to prevent our
seeing it. It is the business of a Commissioner to
separate truth from falsehood, to see things as *they
are*, and to render justice, tempered with lenity, to all.
It is the business of an attorney, if faithful to his trust,
to hold up a false mirror, to represent things as they
are not, "to make the worse appear the better cause,"
to mix the bitter ingredients with disguise, and gild
over the pill, that the Commissioner may swallow it.

A plaintiff sued for 1*l*. 19*s*. 11*d*. An attorney,
appearing for the defendant, asked the plaintiff,
whether he held the defendant's note of hand? He
then produced one of ten guineas, payable by instalments, more than two guineas of which was due, and
observed, the money he now sued for was no part of
the note, but a separate debt. The attorney remarked
the note was not valid, no consideration having been
given, but was fraudulently obtained; that if the
matter was examined, a scene of iniquity would open

that would astonish the Bench; that familiarities were supposed to have taken place between the defendant and the plaintiff's wife, and that the ten-guinea note was squeezed out of the defendant as hush-money.

Court: The validity of the note perhaps may be known by investigating the affair. If it should appear collusion had been practised by an artful husband and deceitful wife, to draw in and fleece an innocent person, we should instantly quash the proceedings, and destroy the security. But if it should appear the defendant formed and executed his own plan, that he deliberately trampled down the fences of virtue, invaded the premises, and gathered the fruits, solely the property of another, we should consider it as *value received*. No man ought to take property without reparation. If, by this ten-guinea note, he stifles a prosecution of *crim. con.* he is perhaps a gainer by the contract, and favour from us, without justice, is not to be expected; we would distribute both. But as it is an established maxim in this Court never to throw down a stumbling reputation, but to give it every chance of recovering itself, we shall at present, having dropped these hints to the suitors, for their reconciliation, forbear the enquiry. We would remark to the plaintiff that an order cuts off every claim from the beginning of the world to the issuing of the summons. If the debt is just, he will, by a decision, lose three pounds, which he seems not aware of. For these reasons it is his interest to withdraw the action, and as the note is payable *to order*, endorse it to another; for every holder has a right of suit, in which case he may, if the affair cannot be compromised, sue for his 1*l.* 19*s.* 11*d.* and the note may also be recovered.

The Second Part.

Matters between the contending parties not being settled, and they having launched into the troubled ocean of law, without daring a voyage, the plaintiff, a fortnight after, brought again his cause, his note, and his evidence.

The evidence declared, " that he went to the plaintiff's house, who took him into the cellar: hearing a noise above, the plaintiff desired him to peep through a chink in the door, when he saw the defendant put his arms round the wife's waist, and move with her towards the wall. She called to her husband for help, who rushed in, swore like a coal-heaver, turned the wife out, fastened the door, seized the poker, and bullied the defendant, trembling for his skin and his character, out of the ten-guinea note."

The plaintiff contended, with chagrin in his face and fire in his eye, that the defendant had *offered* him two guineas, which he refused, that he had a just title to the note, that it was fairly obtained, and that the other had no right to take liberties with his wife.

Court: And so you suppose a simple embrace of your wife worth ten guineas! You must suppose yourself immensely rich possessed of such a treasure! Why then do you press money out of the unwary? If a man is liable to a ten-guinea tax for so trifling a liberty he has reason to dread a tax, even for a look; what then must be the price of possession! But perhaps, for the money charged here, you had rather she was encircled with the arms of another than your own. You say the note was freely written; you should rather say it was written with the poker. Though the freedoms taken by the defendant may not always be justified by the perfect rules of decorum, yet, we apprehend, they rather merit a reprimand than a fine.

As far as we have stated the case, you can have no demand; but, perhaps, if we examine three little incidents, which occurred in the trial, you will appear in a diabolical light. Taking your evidence into the cellar carries with it all the formality of design. Your wife calling for help was meant to proclaim her innocence, and convey notice to you. Why then did you turn her out of door? It could only be to save appearances; these indicate it a preconcerted plan between you; and her afterwards remarking to a neighbour, " we have nabbed the defendant," confirms it. How base must be that husband who can prostitute the mind of his wife! There is but one step more in his power, and that he can easily surmount, to prostitute her person. The wife, too, who condescends to league with her husband to deceive one man, will league with another to deceive him. We were totally unacquainted with the merits of the cause when last before us, and gave you a chance of saving your credit, but your extreme desire of money, and that not your own, has induced you publicly to expose yourselves in a degrading light, has nipped your profits in the bud, blasted your future views, and brought a stain upon your reputation, which nothing but time can wash out.

XXXVII.

THE COLLECTOR.

I HAVE remarked that every contested cause has
two sides, supported by two antagonists, each believ-
ing himself right, is entitled to victory; but as only one
can succeed, the other becomes chagrined. If he is an
inferior he will plentifully discharge his abuse at the
Commissioner, behind his back; if an equal, perhaps
accuse him to his face; so that whether he determines
right or wrong he cannot escape censure. But as a
mind oppressed with loss can only find relief in words,
and as words hurt nothing, except a man chooses to
be hurt by them, the Commissioner, who has acted to
the best of his powers, may as well let them pass with
a smile. The use of the tongue being all that is left to
the loser, it would be cruel to deprive him of that last,
cheap, and desirable remedy.

A collector of the King's taxes, not being paid by
about six persons, while in office, had, to make up
his accounts, paid the money for them, and brought
them to the Court for repayment.

The Commissioners were surprised, as no cause of
this nature had ever come before them, and it seemed
of consequence. They enquired how far he was
authorised to pay for another? He answered, he had
paid for some at their own request, with a promise
to be reimbursed; but in other cases, unrequested by
the debtor; that it was done out of kindness to them,
to prevent a distress, and as the money was paid out
of his own pocket, it was reasonable he should have
it returned.

Court: All public taxes are debts due from private persons to the Crown; how highly then is this little Court honoured when our aid is requested to assist the *King* in recovering his debts! The same honour awaits you, who stand before us as the representative of majesty! Instead of this being a Court of Equity, one would think it a Court of Falsehood, for unfor-- tunately we can scarcely believe half what is said to the Bench. It is not our business to enquire into *motives*, but *facts*, otherwise it might appear doubtful whether the spring of action was *their* interest, or your own. Though at a transient view all your debts may appear of one aspect, yet upon a close inspection they will be found of two distinct natures. Where the debtor requested you to lay down the money, or pro-- mised payment, you have a right to the debt, and we shall award it with pleasure; it was an act of kindness which merits the thanks of the debtor; it was a fair contract between two parties, which we have no right to dissolve. But where you paid, without that request, you paid it in your own wrong, and must sustain the loss. To give you such a debt would draw after it a numerous catalogue of evils. It is giving instability to property, taking that power out of those hands where alone it should rest, and conferring it on him who has no right to receive it. No man can pay my money without my consent. If this was allowed, I am no longer my own master, for if he has a right to pay one debt, he has a right to pay any, or even all, and as very few people can instantly answer every demand, without breaking the line they wish to preserve, he brings me to that ruin which prudence cannot shun, he lays a trap which all my foresight cannot avoid. This liberty, though in the form of a kindness, brings destruction in its rear, and is a liberty one man has no right to take with another. The debtor is the best judge what debts are necessary to be discharged first. As he is the responsible man, he ought to be the acting one. What prudent Court then would introduce and license a destructive meddler? If we leave the door open, what mischiefs may not enter! and if admitted, where can we stop them? The master must give way to the intruder, while the secrets of trade, the concerns of the family, and the mysteries of the counting-house are laid open to view. The law has marked out a road for the collector, by distress, and this road he is obliged to follow; he cannot mark out one for himself.

At this important trial we were three Commissioners upon the Bench; two of them were at first, from motives of gratitude, inclined to decide for the collector; but, for the reasons above, we were unanimous for the defendant; consequently the wrath of the collector, and that of his friends, fell upon me. Some, who were disinterested, approved the decision, but which was right must be left to the world.

XXXVIII.

THE HUNTED JEW.

It is rather strange for a Jew to turn Christian; stranger still to turn Christian preacher; and yet more strange if we find him a *Methodist* preacher. All this happened to Philip Levi Coan, who having renounced the Jewish faith, became an object of detestation to the Jews. Pelted, hooted, hissed at by his forsaken

brethren, nothing but the restraining laws of England
could preserve his life. Every art was put in practice
to ruin him. All his past errors, whether real or
imaginary, were held up to view, while he considered
himself the persecuted apostle of the Gentiles. As he
possessed all the perseverance and the poverty of an
apostle they were determined he should, like them,
preach to none but prisoners, therefore fabricated a
debt of nine shillings and sixpence for shirt pins, sold
many years before at Bristol, and brought him to the
Court of Requests.

There is a persecuting spirit in man, which may be
softened by education, but can never be eradicated.
This spirit, like its father Satan, can change
itself into many forms, and operate as many ways,
but chiefly against those whose country, or religion,
differ from our own. We often find this spirit changed
into an angel of light, for the persecutor has always
the address to cover his actions with " the cause of the
Almighty," "fighting the battles of the Lord," doing
" God service." But are our ideas of a Divine power
just when we suppose He cannot proceed without our
aid? Pride tells us our help is necessary, but reason
contradicts it. Perhaps this angel of light appeared
when Moses butchered the Egyptian, and covered his
crime in the sand. The same active spirit was, for a
while, laid with Pharaoh in the Red Sea, but revived
again in Joshua, when he destroyed whole nations who
had never offended him; for though the character of
this hero stands without spot in our day, it did not
stand fair in his own, for we read that the persecuted,
who escaped his sword, flying towards the east of the
Mediterranean, erected a pillar, which, many ages
after, was discovered, with this inscription, " We flee

from Joshua, the son of *Noune*, the robber." It appeared in Elisha, when he commanded his sister savages to devour forty-two children, who had only acted like children, when a smile and a kiss would have stopped their childish ridicule, and established peace for ever. Perhaps he was a bachelor, and a stranger to parental affection. It has haunted the Jewish Church to the present day, and it appeared in the suitors before us.

The greatest Man we read of, who cast out many evil spirits, did not cast out this. His design was not to alter human nature, but improve it. He did not choose to do the work Himself, but commanded others; for this purpose He has left the most perfect directions and examples that exist; not how a man shall reduce his neighbour's spirit, but his own. How well they have been attended to may be seen by the progress of persecution in the Christian Church. I am not selecting the Jews as the only people with whom this evil spirit abode, for it has been as familiar with the Christians, and has taught us to dye our characters in blood.

A man's conduct can divide itself only into two parts, that towards his Maker and his neighbour. All matters of faith and modes of religious conduct fall under the first head. These matters lie between heaven and the man; another has no right to interfere, neither has *he* a right to obtrude them. What if he should believe that even Satan himself, out of his own materials, forged the fiery chariot for Elijah, and became one of the horses that flew away with him, wherein am I hurt by his belief? and if I am no way injured, with what pretence can I punish him? Certainly I am doing him a diskindness who never did me one. As his faith does not affect me, I have no

powers of control.   If we have a right to punish a man
because he is an infidel, we have a right to punish him
if he is anything else, for we shall always take the
liberty to judge.   Neither can it be a disgrace to a
man to change his religion; it is rather in his favour,
for it shews, at least, that he has thought for himself.
He has the same right to decline a profession as his
ancestor to embrace it.   On the other hand, no man is
to be injured by the conduct of another, otherwise the
laws of his country must interfere.   True liberty consists in thinking and acting as he pleases, but hurting
none.   While he does this he ought to be out of the
reach of law, and of man.

May 26, 1786, a singular figure appeared before
the Bench, under the name of Philip Levi Coan,
dressed in black, rather dirty, about twenty-eight,
remarkably thin, five feet six, with a sallow aspect,
a piercing eye, and a large Hebrew Bible under his
coat.   By his appearance we thought him unable to
speak, but soon found we were unable to silence him.
Samson might have more strength, but he had not
better lungs.   The plaintiff himself was one of the
most voluble speakers that ever appeared in this Court;
perhaps he was chosen out of the tribes for this trial,
but he had no more chance with the preacher than the
Philistines had with Samson, though equally armed
with jawbones.   He accused the Israelites of great
enormities, in as severe terms as the apostles had done
before him, and attempted to preach Christ crucified
to the Bench.

It is in vain to silence a man who is full of wrath
and of words; after he has disburdened himself a little
of both, then is the time to step in.   When the Commissioners observed an opening they remarked—

You are yet but " almost a Christian," for you have
one of its precepts to learn, that of *meekness*.   You
are nearly as great a stranger to this virtue as your
brother teachers in the Christian Church; neither would
it disgrace a Jew if your antagonist, the plaintiff,
infused a little into *his* conduct.   Whether a Jew turns
Christian, or a Christian turns Pagan, is of no consequence to us; we wish to treat you both with justice,
as men, and as brethren.   But wherever we meet with
a persecuting spirit, whether it appears as an angel
of light or an imp of darkness, we shall employ our
little interest to oppose it.   Though we leave the arts
of preaching to you, we shall beg leave to make an
application to this important subject.   It will consist
of two short lessons; one of them is learnt by some,
but neither will by you: Live friendly in future; and
allow another that liberty you wish to take yourselves.

Though your language is nearly unintelligible,
from the broken English united with the broken
Hebrew, and the violence with which both are
delivered, yet we can discover the debt has no foundation but revenge; we shall therefore dismiss the cause
after full hearing to prevent that persecuting spirit,
which cannot prevent itself.

The preacher afterwards declared to his friends
that " he verily believed the Bench were under the
peculiar influence of heaven," which some people, by
the way, rather doubt.

8

XXXIX.

A PICTURE OF MAN FROM THE LIFE.

TITLE and possession, like parent and infant, should ever be united; but if they are separated by rascality or misfortune, every Court, particularly that of Equity, should promote a re-union.

If a *man* loses his purse, containing his whole fortune, he probably will follow it with a few execrations; if a *woman*, with tears. The oaths may recoil upon the giver, the tears may soften the heart, but the Court alone can recover the property.

A man may resolve to methodise his concerns so that the business of an unprofitable office shall not perpetually clash with his own; but pity may disarm his resolution. A woman accosted me with tears, the most powerful emollients in nature, and observed with extreme sorrow that she had lost her needle-book, containing five shillings and sixpence, all she had in the world, in consequence of which her children were starving for bread; that the man who had found it refused to return it, but cursed her, and claimed it for his own; she wished to know whether the Court could relieve her, for if it could not an abortive suit would add to her loss. I remarked in reply that I had not foresight enough to resolve her question, and if I had prudence forbade it; that as I should probably be upon the Bench I could not give advice without being myself culpable; that the event of a cause was uncertain, but if she brought it to the Court the Commissioners would do her all the justice in their power; and, were the case my own, I would not tamely submit to the loss.

At the trial the defendant boldly supported his claim to the property. He had fairly found it, and every thing a man finds is his own.

Court: And so you apprehend the street gives a title to whatever lies upon it? You forget that property cannot change its owner without an act of that owner. You can inherit no title but from her, and she has given you none. If you accidentally find a person's title-deeds, will it give you a right to the estate? Should a man take up your watch, would you think he had a right to keep it? Or rather, would not you hold forth in a different style, and proclaim that power right which obliged him to restore it. It may be generous to reward the finder, but he can demand nothing; neither has the person who wishes to conceal, or refuses to return, what he finds a right to expect a gratuity; we are sorry that half this is your case. A gentleman, some years back, was travelling in Nottinghamshire with a servant, who carried a portmanteau, in which was 2,000*l.* to pay for an estate. By some accident it slipped unperceived off the horse. When the loss was discovered the servant posted back. An old woman with the portmanteau on her head, whom they had lately passed, exclaimed, " I know what you are galloping after; here is the treasure you lost; take it and welcome." She was afterwards introduced to the master, who gave her five guineas. Both parties were pleased; and whenever his affairs led him to Nottingham he sent for the old woman, and always gave her a kiss and a guinea; each had a different relish, but both were very acceptable.

An old woman is unjustly deemed a despicable character, but how amiable would yours appear

could it be placed in the same light. Had you been
the fortunate finder, you would have instantly quitted
the road, deposited the prize in a ditch, and covered
it, as the robin redbreast did the babes in the wood,
with leaves, till the darkness of the night should favour
the thief to carry off the property of another.

We shall allow you what you do not deserve—one
shilling; make an order against you for the rest, and
leave you to reflect how you *stand* with the world, and
how you *might* have stood. Had you sought out the
loser, freely returned the property without a fee, for
she wanted and you did not, you would have stood
upon honourable ground. You may further reflect
that your *honesty* will never be called in question,
for of this you have publicly made shipwreck; your
capacity may, for as every loser of a cause pays the
fees, you have for twelve paltry pence bartered away
seventeen and a character.

XL.

THE NECESSITY OF MARRYING.

No man can justify drawing to himself the property
of another. No Court ought to allow it. Should a
man get possession of the heart of a woman, it does
not give him a title to her money; nay, should they
grant each other all the privileges the two sexes can
grant, it no way unites their property; their effects,
like their persons, are two, and marriage alone can
make them one.

In some cases I have mentioned the real names of
the parties, but in others, where it might have been

imprudent, or where they were forgotten, I have adopted that antiquated subterfuge practised by the libelist and the lawyer of calling in the letters of the alphabet to personify the characters.

Let us suppose, then, A to represent a servant girl of twenty-seven, B a book-keeper about the same age, C an apprentice boy of eighteen learning the art of gunmaking, all inmates in the same family.

A, having found it too difficult to live twenty-seven years without a man, had admitted to her embraces B and C, but whether she had admitted the whole alphabet did not appear. A pregnancy was the result; consequently a husband must be found. But whether she had admitted the whole alphabet, or only a part, was not material, for it could no more be ascertained which was the father than which was the effective bullet that kills when a platoon fires at a deserter.

She might be said, however, to be mistress of the A, B, C, for they, being in her power, she could lead or drive them at pleasure. She expanded the marriage lure for B, but he was too shy to be caught. In a gay humour B displayed two guineas in his open hand; A in the same humour snatched them out; "she should soon have occasion for them," with a smile. *He* regretted, wished, hinted, asked. She smiled again, acquiesced, and even promised, but still kept the money.

As no time could be lost, she married C, and refused to pay the two guineas, alleging it was a present.

All debts contracted by a woman before marriage must be sued for in the name of both. B brought this to the Court in the name of C and A his wife. C pleaded his nonage.

The Court allowed the debt might be just, but they could not give it B, for though the woman was of age when the debt was contracted, and liable to the sentence of the Court, yet, becoming a wife, she is protected by her husband; she cannot be separated from him. Neither can their sentence reach the husband, because of his minority. Had it been contracted by himself, it would have been lost for ever; but, being contracted in the adult state of the wife, a responsibility will revive in him when he becomes an adult himself.

XLI.

THE NECESSITY OF UNMARRYING.

It is happy, in the economy of man, that one power can control another throughout the whole system of government. If a suitor thinks himself injured in one Court, he can fly to another. This will excite a Court, for its own credit, to endeavour after justice, that the suitor may have no *occasion* to fly. A Judge is apt to feel himself awkward when his sentence is reversed by the Chancellor, and the Chancellor may feel himself hurt when his decree is reversed by the Lords; nay, even the Lords decide with caution, for the eye of the world is upon them. If the defaulter appears before that little tribunal, the Court of Conscience, the Commissioners themselves must appear before the greatest tribunal we know—*the public.*

Though I have given many examples of the conduct of the Bench, I can only hold myself responsible for those I approved. If I am outvoted, the cause is not

mine, though I describe it.   I am no more accountable
than a woman whose virtue is forced.   Of this description is *the oppressed suitor*, who was deprived of his
right; *the merchant and the button-maker*, where the
former was charged a guinea, though it was easy to
see he was before a loser.   Had the decision been with
me, I would have awarded a trifle to end the contest;
also, in the case, *the power of beauty*, I would have
obliged the landlady to refund the money she took,
had her charms been twice as many.   If a man receives
favours, they are for himself, and ought to be paid
for out of his own property; but if he robs the temple
of equity, it becomes the greatest evil of the two.   I
was highly pleased with the reply of a Lord Chancellor
to one of his mistresses, who strongly interested herself
in favour of a clergyman to fill a vacant benefice.   " At
all events, Madam, I shall provide for you, but I hold
it a duty to confer emoluments upon merit, and of that
I shall be judge.   Therefore let me have no more of
your solicitations."

I am, however, of opinion there are cases where
the barriers of justice may be broken through.   A debt
may be acknowledged on both sides, and yet the Bench
may be justified in depriving the owner.   I have given
an example in case the fifth.

As our marriage-makers are fond of being well
paid, if they could erect *a court for the dissolution of
marriage*, it would *almost* pay them to their wish.   If
their price was easy, their custom would be immense !
No Court would be more useful, not even that I
describe.   It would now and then save half a pair
from being knocked on the head, and the other half
from being hanged.   It would be serviceable, even
where matters are not carried to extremes, by preserv-

ing order in the family. The husband durst not act imprudently, lest the wife should apply; it would also silence *her* tongue, which nothing yet could silence, for fear of offending the husband. If this *Court of dissolution* could not introduce love, it could peace. Their fear of the Court might enforce that decent behaviour, which in time would grow into a habit.

Should it be objected that this doctrine is contrary to Scripture, which says, " Those whom God has joined together, let no man put asunder," it may be asked, If the Almighty makes every match, whether He has not made some of them very ill? And whether those of the Fleet and Gretna Green are chargeable to His account? If it should be said He only makes a part, how can we distinguish? Probably it is that part which would have no occasion for the *Court of dissolution*. Should it again be objected that to dissolve the marriage knot is dangerous, it may be further asked, What evil can arise from untying a knot which the proprietors are resolved to cut asunder?

Two young men, decent in appearance, came before the Bench. One demanded thirty-nine shillings and elevenpence. When this is the claim we reasonably suppose the debt more. The other acknowledged it right, but thought it cruel to pay, for the plaintiff had taken from him his wife.

Court: Did you take her?

Plaintiff: Yes.

C.: Do you keep her now?

P.: Yes, I bought her.

C.: We did not know Birmingham was a market for wives. We considered its market designed for a wife's support, not her sale. By the external accomplishments of both she has made an inferior choice. Upon what do you found the debt?

P. : He owes me four pounds, which was money I advanced to his wife when they cohabited together.

C. : You seem to have had a prior connection with her, or why did you supply her with money? Perhaps that money was to draw her affections, and prepare her for your own purpose; consequently it operated to the husband's destruction. Should you think it right to be obliged to pay for the pistol with which a rascal robbed you? She is as much his wife now as before, and you might with as much propriety sue for her board.

Clerk of the Court : If he takes the woman, he ought to take her debts.

P. : He owes me the money, and if you will not allow it the cause shall be dismissed out of this Court that I may recover it in another.

C. : If you will restore the wife in the same state you found her, we will order you the debt.

The husband seemed to feel his own distress; his eye reddened, the indication of a rising tear. What dreadful devastations are made by misconduct in the married state when unguarded by prudence!

You cannot repair the mischief already done, yet wish to do more. In what light shall we view that temper which would do a man a second injury merely because he had done him a first? You have ruined the wife, and now thirst after the husband. You have extracted the small remains of prudence, love, and peace, the sweetest ingredients in the matrimonial cup, and infused poison in their stead, which has converted it into a bitter draught. Our powers are too feeble to restore a roving wife, nor, without repentance, is she worth it. Her prudence never existed, her affections are extinct, so is her pity, or you durst not have prosecuted this suit; but our powers are able to cut off your revenge, and restore a small degree of peace to an afflicted husband by charging him with a debt of *one shilling*.

The plaintiff seemed greatly disappointed, and the husband pleased to find some relief in a friendly Court.

XLII.

THE FORSAKEN FAIR.

SHOULD a case between two contentious people appear plain, it would be easy to pronounce upon it; no motive but justice should influence the Bench. But if a disputable case arises between a young fellow, as full of ill-nature as a hag of seventy, and a beautiful girl, possessing the accomplishments of person, affability, dress, and modesty, it is easy to guess on which side the scale would incline. In the first instance, the judgment of a Commissioner is tied to an unalterable rule; but in the second, it expands to a more extensive latitude. There is a material difference between a declaration from mildness and one from revenge, and still more between a fact *asserted* and *proved*.

There is not in the whole creation a more pleasing picture than a beautiful woman; none that will so much impress the beholder. Even the man of sixty, who has no pretensions but to admire, steals a look with pleasure, and regrets the loss of twenty-five.

Although features, figure, complexion, and dress are *four* leading powers to form a beauty, yet five are as necessary as her five senses. She is incomplete without a peculiar softness, easily discovered in the face, felt in the heart, but not easily described. Airs of pride dissipate the effects of beauty.

The Bench were surprised when a handsome young man, of genteel appearance, brought before them a young woman much handsomer, who seemed to merit the above description, and behaved to her with all the acrimony that revenge could dictate. The Commissioners soon perceived they had been lovers, but did not know the cause of their separation, and delicacy prevented the enquiry.

As a woman of this class stands upon slippery ground, the Bench were apprehensive of a declaration injurious to her honour; but from a collection of odd shillings he had only fabricated a debt of one pound six, which he pretended to have lent her at various times during their intimacy, and demanded with violence the assistance of the Bench to punish her.

They replied that the *protection* of the fair, and not their punishment, should be his province; that he could not neglect superlative charms, nor suffer them to fall into the arms of another; that a decision would avail nothing, for the quarrel of a lover was only the quarrel of a day, which would disappear before any decision could take effect, when both parties would unite in laughing at the folly of the Commissioners. But their surprise increased when they were given to understand that he had discarded her and married another. This induced them silently to conclude the wife might have poisoned his ear, as Eve did that of

Adam. The case seemed uncommon, for if revenge operates at all it originates from the forsaken party.

She asserted he had frequently treated her to places of amusement, but never on any account advanced her money. A witness to a conversation between them declared that he threatened her with a suit in this Court; that he would swear to the debt, and if he could not recover it there would pursue her through every Court under the Crown till he could. That she answered she owed him nothing, and if he swore to the debt he would take a false oath; but he replied he would take twenty rather than miss his revenge.

The cause inclining against him, he boldly charged the Bench with injustice, asserting they had privately prejudged it before its appearance in public; insisted upon taking it out of Court, and carrying it to another, where he could have that justice denied him here; but the Court remarked:

As you voluntarily put the cause into our hands, it rests with us to dispose of it as we think right. Instead of a prejudgment, we are not conscious that we ever saw either of you before. Whether any private transactions between you have inflamed your diabolical temper, and sunk you beneath a man, is also unknown to us; nor do we wish to enquire. But if the debt was just on one side and denied on the other, it could not merit the treatment you give. For many reasons, however, we think it spurious; she does not seem to stand in need of a twelve-penny boon. The evidence is much against you; but the principal is, whatever favours passed between you were meant to be *given*. Therefore, no change of sentiment or of circumstance can convert them into a debt. We shall, for once, deliver the lamb from the lion, *dismiss the cause after full hearing*, which will for ever muzzle your savage fangs; and though you will not thank us, we shall preserve your property and your reputation from being lost in another Court.

But if one debt ought to bear a speedier payment than another, it might be asked whether we should not imitate our ministers and charge this payment upon luxuries, as drinking, hairdressing, horse hire, &c., which a man might do without. But perhaps the Commissioner may as well rest satisfied if he can acquire two informations—the justice of the debt and the ability of the debtor.

In every institution there are some general rules which, like fundamental laws, should ever be kept in view. When these are observed they methodise proceedings, facilitate business, the Court wears a fair and easy aspect, the suitors are preserved from injustice, and the Commissioners from disgrace. I shall take the liberty of introducing a few under the name of

MAXIMS FOR THE BENCH.

1. Avoid hearing one party, except the other is by.
2. Beware of being biased by the first speaker.
3. Procure all the information possible from both, but lean to neither.
4. Assist *him* to regain his property who has lost it.
5. Promote peace between contending parties.
6. If a suitor has formerly offended in his private capacity, never carry resentment to the Bench.
7. Let the Commissioner for a moment suppose himself in the place of each of the opponents; this will often furnish him with the clue to justice.

8. Allow all necessary time to sift a case to the bottom; but when once master of the subject close it, that time may be saved and the repeated arguments of the parties cease.

9. Put an end to the contest, though the evidence is doubtful, if it can be done with a degree of justice, lest the angry parties tear each other to pieces in another Court.

10. Give the loser a reason why he ought to lose, otherwise a decision will assume an arbitrary face.

11. Let every defendant pay the debt as soon as he conveniently can.

12. Though the Statute of Limitations is necessary, yet as time pays no debts, let the weight of the Bench operate against him who pleads it.

13. Consider what consequences will attend a determination.

14. Power should never oppress; let the Commissioner use his, which is great, for the benefit of every individual except himself.

But notwithstanding all his care, errors of judgment will attend him, as appears by the following case.

XLIII.

BETTY JOHN.

A PLAINTIFF wished to sue a person in this Court, but not knowing whether the party was male or female was at a loss by what name to begin. The defendant had been many years known in Birmingham, in the dress and character of a woman, called Elizabeth, and had been many years known in the dress and character of a man, who answered to the name of John. The plaintiff, after many fruitless enquiries, determined to trap the person, let the sex be what it would; therefore filled up the summons with *Elizabeth, alias John Haywood.*

Whatever was the gender, the animal appeared before the Court in a female habit, was rather elegant, of a moderate size, tolerably handsome, about thirty-two, had a firm countenance and manly step, no beard, eyes susceptible of love, a voice tending to the masculine, with manners engaging, and was rather sensible. A husband was pleaded in bar, and that the Court had no power over a wife. The trial continued three or four days, during which the defendant acquired the appellation from the people of *Betty John.* The Court was uncommonly crowded. The women could have pulled its cap, and tossed it in a blanket, for verging upon their sex. The men listened with great attention. Expectation marked every face. As it attended the Court in a female dress, I shall take the liberty of treating it with a feminine epithet.

It appeared from undoubted evidence that while she dressed like a man, she was suspected to be a woman, but in both dresses was strongly suspected to be a man. The common opinion of the ignorant, who knew her, was that she was an hermaphrodite, partaking of both sexes; an animal never yet known, notwithstanding Knighton, Grafton, &c. tell us, " That in 1246 there was a woman in the diocese of Lincoln, of noble birth, well favoured and beautiful, which was married to a rich man, and did bear him children; she also got another gentlewoman with child, and begat three sons of her, one after another, or ever it was known; their names were Havissia and Lucia." But the age in which these ladies lived was marked with credulity, every ear was open to wonder; the cunning Miss Lucy, taking advantage of this weakness, might attempt to shelter her lover and her reputation under the petticoat.

While the defendant carried a male dress, she spent her evenings at the public with her male companions, and could, like them, swear with a tolerable grace, get drunk, smoke tobacco, kiss the girls, and now and then kick a bully. Though she pleaded being a wife, she had really been a husband; for she courted a young woman, married her, and they lived together in wedlock till the young woman died, which was some years after, and without issue. She afterwards, like the people of higher rank, kept a mistress, and ran away with her.

Forcible evidences, like these, were sufficient to convince the wisest head upon this Bench, or any other, that a man in disguise stood before them. Her wife living peaceably with her all her days, without one complaint of a breach of the marriage covenant, evinced there was no defect. Neither would a girl sacrifice her reputation by becoming a mistress to a woman in breeches; this would be changing the sub-

stance for the shadow.   Besides, a woman receives
very little more pleasure in saluting a living woman
than a dead one; whereas a man, like the figure before
the Bench, seemed to receive a pleasure inexpressible.
Her being well versed in the art of kicking, further
proved she was a man, because it is an art never
thoroughly understood by the beautiful part of the
creation, nor has it been practised since the days of
Queen Elizabeth.   Again, she spoke but little, which
was no indication of her being a woman.

Under these masculine proofs the Court, not convinced she was a wife, asked if she could produce any
evidence of her being married? She answered in the
affirmative. This evidence, the next Court-day, only
went to prove that a man had lived with her in the
capacity of a husband.   But as instances might be
produced of a man and woman cohabiting together
without being married, the plea was rejected.   She
was further asked, if she could bring a certificate of
her marriage? She would try.

The certificate, on a future day, was produced, but,
like a Birmingham bill drawn without effects, it passed
from hand to hand for inspection, but was returned
with great indifference, without an acceptance.   A
scrap of paper, it was observed, containing a few simple
words, might, like a gipsy's brat, be brought forth
under any hedge, or drawn by a penny from a school-
boy.

The Court, not satisfied she was a wife, and no
further evidence arising, entered an order against her.
On her neglecting payment she was served with an
execution, and committed to prison. Two days after
it appeared from incontestable proof that she was a real
woman, and a real wife; that her husband then resided

9

in Shropshire, and that she had nothing of the man about her higher than the feet.

The Commissioners, sensible of the injury done her, wished to make reparation; but, alas! their powers were extinct; their determinations, like the events of fate, were unalterable. She cancelled the debt by a confinement of forty days.

In the case before us law and equity, which should ever be the same, militated against each other. The law would have acquitted the defendant, though she actually contracted the debt. It would have charged the husband with the payment, though he was wholly innocent. Perhaps the error committed by the Bench was an error of right; they punished the guilty through mistake, who was acquitted by law, and acquitted the innocent, whom the law would have found guilty.

PART II.

WITCH TRIALS.

INTRODUCTION.

THE trials of the Salem Witches are reprinted from *The Wonders of the Invisible World*, a rare work written by Cotton Mather, and *A Further Account of the Tryals*, by his father, Increase Mather.

The scene of this affair was the puritanical colony of New England, since better known as Massachusetts, the colonists of which appear to have carried with them, in an exaggerated form, the superstitious feelings with regard to witchcraft which then prevailed in the Mother Country. In the spring of 1692 an alarm of witchcraft was raised in the family of the minister of Salem, and some black servants were charged with the supposed crime. Once started, the alarm spread rapidly, and in a very short time a great number of people fell under suspicion, and many were thrown into prison on very frivolous grounds, supported, as such charges usually were, by very unworthy witnesses. The new governor of the colony, Sir William Phipps, arrived from England in the middle of May, and he seems to have been carried away by the excitement, and authorised judicial prosecutions. The trials began at the commencement of June; and the first victim, a woman named Bridget Bishop, was hanged. Governor Phipps, embarrassed by this extraordinary state of things, called in the assistance of the clergy of Boston.

In the summer of the year 1688 the children of a mason of Boston, named John Goodwin, were suddenly seized with fits and strange afflictions, which were at once ascribed to witchcraft, and an Irish washerwoman named Glover, employed by the family, was suspected of being the witch. Cotton Mather was called in to witness the sufferings of Goodwin's children; and he took home with him one of them, a little girl, who had first displayed these symptoms, in order to examine her with more care. The result was that the Irishwoman was brought to a trial, found guilty, and hanged; and Cotton Mather published next year an account of the case, under the title of " Late Memorable Providences, relating to Witchcraft and Possession," which displays a very extraordinary amount of credulity, and an equally great want of anything like sound judgment. This work, no doubt, spread the alarm of witchcraft through the whole colony, and had some influence on the events which followed. It may be supposed that the panic which had now arisen in Salem was not likely to be appeased by the interference of Cotton Mather and his father.

The execution of the washerwoman, Bridget Bishop, had greatly increased the excitement; and people in a more respectable position began to be accused. On the 19th of July five more persons were executed, and five more experienced the same fate on the 19th of August. Among the latter was Mr. George Borroughs, a minister of the Gospel, whose principal crime appears to have been a disbelief in witchcraft itself. His fate excited considerable sympathy, which, however, was checked by Cotton Mather, who was present at the place of execution on horseback, and addressed the crowd, assuring them that Borroughs was an impostor. Many people, however, had now become alarmed at the proceedings of the prosecutors, and among those executed with Borroughs was a man named John Willard, who had been employed to arrest the persons charged by the accusers, and who had been accused himself, because, from conscientious motives, he refused to arrest any more. He attempted to save himself by flight, but he was pursued and overtaken. Eight more of the unfortunate victims of this delusion were hanged on the 22nd of September, making in all nineteen who had thus suffered, besides one who, in accordance with the old criminal law practice, had been pressed to death for refusing to plead. The excitement had indeed risen to such a pitch that two dogs accused of witchcraft were put to death.

A certain degree of reaction, however, appeared to be taking place, and the magistrates who had conducted the proceedings began to be alarmed, and to have some doubts of the wisdom of their proceedings. Cotton Mather was called upon by the Governor to employ his pen in justifying what had been done; and the result was the book, " The Wonders of the Invisible World," in which the author gives an account of seven of the trials at Salem, compares the doings of the witches in New England with those in other parts of the world, and adds an elaborate dissertation on witchcraft in general. This book was published at Boston, Massachusetts, in the month of October, 1692. Other circumstances, however, contributed to throw discredit on the proceedings of the Court, though the witch mania was at the same time spreading throughout the whole

colony. In this same month of October the wife of
Mr. Hale, minister of Beverley, was accused, although
no person of sense and respectability had the slightest
doubt of her innocence; and her husband had been a
zealous promoter of the prosecutions. This accusation
brought a new light on the mind of Mr. Hale, who
became convinced of the injustice in which he had been
made an accomplice; but the other ministers who took
the lead in the proceedings were less willing to believe
in their own error; and equally convinced of the
innocence of Mrs. Hale, they raised a question of conscience, whether the devil could not assume the shape
of an innocent and pious person, as well as of a wicked
person, for the purpose of afflicting his victims. The
assistance of Increase Mather, the president or principal of Harvard College, was now called in, and he
published the book " A Further Account of the Tryals
of the New England Witches. . . . To which is added
Cases of Conscience concerning Witchcrafts and Evil
Spirits personating Men." The greater part of the
" Cases of Conscience " is given to the discussion of
the question just alluded to, which Increase Mather
unhesitatingly decides in the affirmative. The scene
of agitation was now removed from Salem to Andover,
where a great number of persons were accused of
witchcraft and thrown into prison, until a Justice of
the peace named Bradstreet, to whom the accusers
applied for warrants, refused to grant any more.
Hereupon they cried out upon Bradstreet, and declared
that he had killed nine persons by means of witchcraft;
and he was so much alarmed that he fled from the
place. The accusers aimed at people in higher posi-
tions in society, until at last they had the audacity to
cry out upon the lady of Governor Phipps himself, and

thus lost whatever countenance he had given to their proceedings out of respect to the two Mathers. Other people of character, when they were attacked by the accusers, took energetic measures in self-defence. A gentleman of Boston, " when cried out upon," obtained a writ of arrest against his accusers on a charge of defamation, and laid the damages at a thousand pounds. The accusers themselves now took fright, and many who had made confessions retracted them, while the accusations themselves fell into discredit. When Governor Phipps was recalled in April, 1693, and left for England, the witchcraft agitation had nearly subsided, and people in general had become convinced of their error and lamented it.

But Cotton Mather and his father persisted obstinately in the opinions they had published, and looked upon the reactionary feeling as a triumph of Satan and his kingdom. In the course of the year they had an opportunity of reasserting their belief in the doings of the witches of Salem. A girl of Boston, named Margaret Rule, was seized with convulsions, in the course of which she pretended to see the " shapes " or spectres of people exactly as they were alleged to have been seen by the witch-accusers at Salem and Andover. This occurred on the 10th of September, 1693; and she was immediately visited by Cotton Mather, who examined her, and declared his conviction of the truth of her statements. Had it depended only upon him, a new and no doubt equally bitter persecution of witches would have been raised in Boston; but an influential merchant of that town, named Robert Calef, took the matter up in a different spirit, and also examined Margaret Rule, and satisfied himself that the whole was a delusion or imposture. Calef wrote a rational account of the events of these two years, 1692 and 1693, exposing the delusion, and controverting the opinions of the two Mathers on the subject of witchcraft, which was published under the title of " More Wonders of the Invisible World; or the Wonders of the Invisible World displayed in five parts. An Account of the Sufferings of Margaret Rule collected by Robert Calef, merchant of Boston in New England." The partisans of the Mathers displayed their hostility to this book by publicly burning it; and the Mathers themselves kept up the feeling so strongly that years afterwards, when Samuel Mather, the son of Cotton, wrote his father's life, he says sneeringly of Calef: " There was a certain disbeliever in witchcraft who wrote against this book " (his father's " Wonders of the Invisible World "), " but as the man is dead, his book died long before him." Calef died in 1720.

The witchcraft delusion had, however, been sufficiently dispelled to prevent the recurrence of any other such persecutions; and those who still insisted on their truth were restrained to the comparatively harmless publication and defence of their opinions. The people of Salem were humbled and repentant. They deserted their minister, Mr. Paris, with whom the persecution had begun, and were not satisfied until they had driven him away from the place. Their remorse continued through several years, and most of the people concerned in the judicial proceedings proclaimed their regret. The jurors signed a paper expressing their repentance, and pleading that they had laboured under a delusion. What ought to have been considered still more conclusive, many of those who had confessed themselves witches, and had been instrumental in accusing others, retracted all they had said, and confessed that they had acted under the influence of terror. Yet the vanity of superior intelligence and knowledge was so great in the two Mathers that they resisted all conviction. In his " Magnalia," an ecclesiastical history of New England, published in 1700, Cotton Mather repeats his original view of the doings of Satan in Salem, showing no regret for the part he had taken in this affair, and making no retractation of any of his opinions. Still later, in 1723, he repeats them again in the same strain in the chapter of the " Remarkables " of his father, entitled " Troubles from the Invisible World." His father, Increase Mather, had died in that same year at an advanced age, being in his eighty-fifth year. Cotton Mather died on the 13th of February, 1728.

Whatever we may think of the credulity of these two ecclesiastics, there can be no ground for charging them with acting otherwise than conscientiously, and they had claims on the gratitude of their countrymen sufficient to overbalance their error of judgment on this occasion.

The instructions for the discovery of witches immediately following are taken from Cotton Mather's book.

AN ABSTRACT OF MR. PERKINS'S WAY FOR THE DISCOVERY OF WITCHES.

I. THERE are *presumptions*, which do at least probably and conjecturally note one to be a *witch*. These give occasion to examine, yet they are no sufficient causes of conviction.

II. If any man or woman be notoriously defamed for a *witch*, this yields a strong suspicion. Yet the Judge ought carefully to look that the report be made by *men* of honesty and credit.

III. If a *fellow-witch*, or *magician*, give testimony of any person to be a *witch*, this indeed is not sufficient for condemnation; but it is a fit presumption to cause a strait examination.

IV. If after cursing there follow death, or at least some mischief: for *witches* are wont to practise their mischievous facts by cursing and banning. This also is a sufficient matter of examination, though not of conviction.

V. If after enmity, quarrelling, or threatening a present mischief does follow; that also is a great presumption.

VI. If the party suspected be the son or daughter, the man-servant or maid-servant, the familiar friend, near neighbour, or old companion, of a known and convicted witch; this may be likewise a presumption;

for witchcraft is an art that may be learned, and conveyed from man to man.

VII. Some add this for a presumption: If the party suspected be found to have the devil's mark; for it is commonly thought, when the devil makes his covenant with them, he always leaves his mark behind them, whereby he knows them for his own—a mark whereof no evident reason in nature can be given.

VIII. Lastly, if the party examined be unconstant, or contrary to himself, in his deliberate answers, it argueth a guilty conscience, which stops the freedom of utterance. And yet there are causes of astonishment which may befall the good, as well as the bad.

IX. But then there is a *conviction*, discovering the *witch*, which must proceed from just and sufficient proofs, and not from bare presumptions.

X. Scratching of the suspected party, and recovery thereupon, with several other such weak proofs; as also, the floating of the suspected party, thrown upon the water; these proofs are so far from being sufficient that some of them are, after a sort, practices of witchcraft.

XI. The testimony of some wizard, though offering to shew the witch's face in a glass: This, I grant, may be a good presumption to cause a strait examination; but a sufficient proof of conviction it cannot be. If the devil tell the grand jury that the person in question is a witch, and offers withal to confirm the same by oath, should the inquest receive his oath or accusation to condemn the man? Assuredly no. And yet that is as much as the testimony of another wizard, who only by the devil's help reveals the witch.

XII. If a man, being dangerously sick, and like to die upon suspicion, will take it on his death that such a one hath bewitched him, it is an allegation of the same nature, which may move the Judge to examine the party, but it is of no moment for conviction.

XIII. Among the sufficient means of conviction the first is the free and voluntary confession of the crime made by the party suspected and accused after examination. I say not that a bare confession is sufficient, but a confession after due examination, taken upon pregnant presumptions. What needs now more witness or further enquiry?

XIV. There is a second sufficient conviction by the testimony of two witnesses of good and honest report, avouching before the magistrate, upon their own knowledge, these two things : either that the party accused hath made a league with the devil, or hath done some known practice of witchcraft. And *all arguments that do necessarily prove either of these*, being brought by two sufficient witnesses, are of force fully to convince the party suspected.

XV. If it can be proved that the party suspected hath called upon the *devil*, or desired his help, this is a pregnant proof of a league formerly made between them.

XVI. If it can be proved that the party hath entertained a familiar spirit, and had conference with it, in the likeness of some visible creatures; here is evidence of witchcraft.

XVII. If the witnesses affirm upon oath that the suspected person hath done any action or work which necessarily infers a covenant made, as that he hath used enchantments, divined things before they come to pass, and that peremptorily, raised tempests, caused the form of a dead man to appear; it proveth sufficiently that he or she is a *witch*. This is the substance of Mr. Perkins.

" Take next the sum of Mr. Gaule's judgment about the detection of witches. 1. Some tokens for the trial of witches are altogether unwarrantable. Such are the old paganish sign, the witch's long eyes; the tradition of witches not weeping; the casting of the witch into the water, with thumbs and toes tied across; and many more such marks, which if they are to know a witch by, certainly it is no other witch, but the user of them. 2. There are some tokens for the trial of witches, more probable, and yet not so certain as to afford conviction. Such are strong and long suspicion: suspected ancestors, some appearance of fact, the corpse bleeding upon the witch's touch, the testimony of the party bewitched, the supposed witch's unusual bodily marks, the witch's usual cursing and banning, the witch's lewd and naughty kind of life. 3. Some signs there are of a witch more certain and infallible; as first, declining of judicature, or faltering, faulty, unconstant, and contrary answers upon judicial and deliberate examination. Secondly, when upon due enquiry into a person's faith and manners there are found all or most of the causes which produce witchcraft—namely, God forsaking, Satan invading, particular sins disposing; and lastly, a compact completing all. Thirdly, the witch's free confession, together with full evidence of the fact. Confession without fact may be a mere delusion, and fact without confession may be a mere accident. Fourthly, the semblable gestures and actions of suspected witches, with the comparable expressions of affections, which in all witches have been observed and found very much alike. Fifthly, the testimony of the party bewitched, whether pining or dying, together with the joint oaths of sufficient persons that have seen certain prodigious

pranks or feats wrought by the party accused.
4. Among the most unhappy circumstances to convict
a witch one is a maligning and oppugning the word,
work, and worship of God, and by any extraordinary
sign seeking to seduce any from it.   See Deut. xiii. 1,
2; Matt. xxiv. 24; Acts xiii. 8, 10; 2 Tim. iii. 8.   Do
but mark well the places, and for this very property
(of thus opposing and perverting) they are all there
concluded arrant and absolute witches.   5. It is not
requisite that so palpable evidence of conviction should
here come in, as in other more sensible matters; it is
enough if there be but so much circumstantial proof or
evidence as the substance, matter, and nature of such
an abstruse mystery of iniquity will well admit."   [I
suppose he means that whereas in other crimes we look
for more direct proofs, in this there is a greater use
of consequential ones.]   "But I could heartily wish
that the juries were empanelled of the most eminent
physicians, lawyers, and divines that a country could
afford.   In the meantime it is not to be called a tolera-
tion, if witches escape, where conviction is wanting."
To this purpose our Gaule.

I will transcribe a little from one author more; it is
the judicious Bernard of Batcomb, who in his "Guide
to Grand Jurymen," after he has mentioned several
things that are shrewd presumptions of a witch, proceeds to such things as are the convictions of such an
one.   And he says: "A witch in league with the devil is
convicted by these evidences: I. By a witch's mark;
which is upon the baser sort of witches; and this, by the
devils either sucking or touching of them.   Tertullian
says, 'It is the devil's custom to mark his.'   And note
that this mark is insensible, and being pricked it will
not bleed.   Sometimes it is like a teat, sometimes but a

bluish spot, sometimes a red one, and sometimes the flesh sunk; but the witches do sometimes cover them. II. By the witches' words. As when they have been heard calling on, speaking to, or talking of their familiars; or when they have been heard telling of hurt they have done to man or beast; or when they have been heard threatening of such hurt; or if they have been heard relating their transportations. III. By the witches' deeds. As when they have been seen with their spirits, or seen secretly feeding any of their imps; or when there can be found their pictures, poppets, and other hellish compositions. IV. By the witches' ecstasies: with the delight whereof witches are so taken that they will hardly conceal the same; or, however at some time or other, they may be found in them. V. By one or more fellow-witches confessing their own witch-craft and bearing witness against others; if they can make good the truth of their witness, and give sufficient proof of it; as that they have seen them with their spirits; or that they have received spirits from them; or that they can tell when they used witchery-tricks to do harm; or that they told them what harm they had done; or that they can show the mark upon them; or that they have been together in their meetings; and such like. VI. By some witness of God Himself, happening upon the execrable curses of witches upon themselves, praying of God to show some token if they be guilty. VII. By the witches' own confession of giving their souls to the devil." It is no rare thing for witches to confess.

They are considerable things which I have thus recited; and yet it must be with open eyes, kept upon open rules, that we are to follow these things.

I.

THE TRIAL OF G. B.,

AT A COURT OF OYER AND TERMINER, HELD IN SALEM, 1692.

GLAD should I have been if I had never known the name of this man, or never had this occasion to mention so much as the first letters of his name; but the Government requiring some account of his trial to be inserted in this book, it becomes me with all obedience to submit unto the order.

I. This G. B. was indicted for witchcraft, and in the prosecution of the charge against him he was accused by five or six of the bewitched as the author of their miseries; he was accused by eight of the confessing witches as being a head actor at some of their hellish rendezvous, and one who had the promise of being a king in Satan's kingdom, now going to be erected; he was accused by nine persons for extraordinary lifting, and such feats of strength as could not be done without a diabolical assistance; and for other such things he was accused, until about thirty testimonies were brought in against him; nor were these judged the half of what might have been considered for his conviction. However, they were enough to fix the character of a witch upon him according to the rules of reasoning, by the judicious Gaule, in that case directed.

II. The Court being sensible that the testimonies of the parties bewitched, use to have a room among the suspicions or presumptions, brought in against one indicted for witchcraft, there were now heard the testi-

10

monies of several persons, who were most notoriously
bewitched, and every day tortured by invisible hands,
and these now all charged the spectres of G. B. to have
a share in their torments. At the examination of this
G. B. the bewitched people were grievously harassed
with preternatural mischiefs, which could not possibly
be dissembled; and they still ascribed it unto the
endeavours of G. B. to kill them. And now upon the
trial of one of the bewitched persons, testified that in
her agonies a little black-haired man came to her,
saying his name was B., and bidding her set her hand
to a book which he showed unto her, and bragging
that he was a conjurer, above the ordinary rank of
witches, that he often persecuted her with the offer of
that book, saying, " She should be well, and need fear
nobody, if she would but sign it "; but he inflicted cruel
pains and hurts upon her because of her denying so
to do. The testimonies of the other sufferers concurred
with these; and it was remarkable that whereas biting
was one of the ways which the witches used for the
vexing of the sufferers, when they cried out of G. B.
biting them the print of the teeth would be seen on
the flesh of the complainers, and just such a set of
teeth as G. B.'s would then appear upon them, which
could be distinguished from those of some other men's.
Others of them testified that in their torments G. B.
tempted them to go unto a Sacrament, unto which
they perceived him with a sound of trumpet summoning
of other witches, who quickly after the sound would
come from all quarters unto the rendezvous. One of
them, falling into a kind of trance, affirmed that G. B.
had carried her away into a very high mountain, where
he showed her mighty and glorious kingdoms, and
said, " He would give them all to her if she would

write in his book "; but she told him, " They were none of his to give," and refused the motions, enduring of much misery for that refusal.

It cost the Court a wonderful deal of trouble to hear the testimonies of the sufferers, for when they were going to give in their depositions they would for a long time be taken with fits, that made them incapable of saying anything.   The chief Judge asked the prisoner who he thought hindered these witnesses from giving their testimonies?   And he answered, " He supposed it was the devil."   That honourable person replied, " How comes the devil then to be so loth to have any testimony borne against you? " which cast him into very great confusion.

III. It has been a frequent thing for the bewitched people to be entertained with apparitions of ghosts of murdered people, at the same time that the spectres of the witches trouble them.   These ghosts do always affright the beholders more than all the other spectral representations; and when they exhibit themselves they cry out of being murdered by the witchcrafts or other violences of the persons who are then in spectre present.   It is further considered that once or twice these apparitions have been seen by others at the very same time they have shown themselves to the bewitched; and seldom have there been these apparitions but when something unusual or suspected has attended the death of the party thus appearing.   Some that have been accused by these apparitions accosting of the bewitched people, who had never heard a word of any such persons ever being in the world, have upon a fair examination freely and fully confessed the murders of those very persons, although these also did not know how the apparitions had complained of them.

Accordingly several of the bewitched had given in their testimony that they had been troubled with the apparitions of two women, who said that they were G. B.'s two wives, and that he had been the death of them, and that the magistrates must be told of it, before whom if B. upon his trial denied it, they did not know but that they should appear again in Court. Now G. B. had been infamous for the barbarous usage of his two late wives all the country over. Moreover, it was testified the spectre of G. B. threatening of the sufferers, told them he had killed (besides others) Mrs. Lawson and her daughter Ann. And it was noted that these were the virtuous wife and daughter of one at whom this G. B. might have a prejudice for his being serviceable at Salem Village, from whence himself had in ill terms removed some years before; and that when they died, which was long since, there were some odd circumstances about them, which made some of the attendants there suspect something of witchcraft, though none imagined from what quarter it should come.

Well, G. B., being now upon his trial, one of the bewitched persons was cast into horror at the ghost of B.'s two deceased wives then appearing before him, and crying for vengeance against him. Hereupon several of the bewitched persons were successively called in, who all not knowing what the former had seen and said, concurred in their horror of the apparition, which they affirmed that he had before him. But he, though much appalled, utterly denied that he discerned anything of it; nor was it any part of his conviction.

IV. Judicious writers have assigned it a great place in the conviction of witches, when persons are im-

peached by other notorious witches, to be as ill as
themselves, especially if the persons have been much
noted for neglecting the worship of God. Now, as there
might have been testimonies enough of G. B.'s antipathy
to prayer, and the other ordinances of God, though by
his profession singularly obliged thereunto, so there
now came in against the prisoner the testimonies of
several persons, who confessed their own having been
horrible witches, and ever since their confessions
have been themselves terribly tortured by the devils
and other witches, even like the other sufferers; and
therein undergone the pains of many deaths for their
confessions.

These now testified that G. B. had been at witch-
meetings with them, and that he was the person who
had seduced and compelled them into the snares of
witchcraft. That he promised them fine clothes for
doing it; that he brought poppets to them, and thorns
to stick into those poppets, for the afflicting of other
people; and that he exhorted them with the rest of the
crew to bewitch all Salem Village, but be sure to do
it gradually if they would prevail in what they did.

When the Lancashire witches were condemned, I
do not remember that there was any considerable
further evidence than that of the bewitched, and than
that of some that confessed. We see so much already
against G. B. But this being indeed not enough, there
were other things to render what had been already
produced credible.

V. A famous divine recites this among the convictions of a witch : The testimony of the party bewitched,
whether pining or dying, together with the joint oaths
of sufficient persons that have seen certain prodigious
pranks or feats wrought by the party accused. Now,

God had been pleased so to leave this G. B. that he had ensnared himself by several instances, which he had formerly given of a preternatural strength, and which were now produced against him. He was a very puny man, yet he had often done things beyond the strength of a giant. A gun of about seven-foot barrel, and so heavy that strong men could not steadily hold it out with both hands : there were several testimonies given in by persons of credit and honour that he made nothing of taking up such a gun behind the lock, with but one hand, and holding it out like a pistol at arm's-end. G. B. in his vindication was so foolish as to say, That an Indian was there, and held it out at the same time : Whereas none of the spectators ever saw any such Indian; but they supposed the black man (as the witches call the devil, and they generally say he resembles an Indian) might give him that assistance. There was evidence likewise brought in that he made nothing of taking up whole barrels filled with molasses or cider in very disadvantageous postures, and carrying of them through the difficultest places out of a canoe to the shore.

Yea, there were two testimonies, that G. B., with only putting the forefinger of his right hand into the muzzle of a heavy gun, a fowling-piece of about six or seven foot barrel, did lift up the gun, and hold it out at arm's-end—a gun which the deponents thought strong men could not with both hands lift up, and hold out at the butt-end, as is usual. Indeed, one of these witnesses was over-persuaded by some persons to be out of the way upon G. B.'s trial, but he came afterwards with sorrow for his withdrawal, and gave in his testimony; nor were either of these witnesses made use of as evidences in the trial.

VI. There came in several testimonies relating to
the domestic affairs of G. B., which had a very hard
aspect upon him, and not only proved him a very ill
man, but also confirmed the belief of the character
which had been already fastened on him.

It was testified that, keeping his two successive
wives in a strange kind of slavery, he would, when
he came home from abroad, pretend to tell the talk
which any had with them; that he has brought them
to the point of death by his harsh dealings with his
wives, and then made the people about him to promise
that, in case death should happen, they would say
nothing of it; that he used all means to make his wives
write, sign, seal, and swear a covenant never to reveal
any of his secrets; that his wives had privately complained unto the neighbours about frightful apparitions
of evil spirits, with which their house was sometimes
infested; and that many such things have been
whispered among the neighbourhood.   There were
also some other testimonies relating to the death of
people, whereby the consciences of an impartial jury
were convinced that G. B. had bewitched the persons
mentioned in the complaints.   But I am forced to
omit several passages in this, as well as in all the
succeeding trials, because the scribes who took notice
of them have not supplied me.

VII. One Mr. Ruck, brother-in-law to this G. B.,
testified that G. B., and himself, and his sister, who
was G. B.'s wife, going out for two or three miles
to gather strawberries, Ruck, with his sister, the wife
of G. B., rode home very softly, with G. B. on foot
in their company.   G. B. stepped aside a little into
the bushes; whereupon they halted and halloo'd for
him.   He not answering, they went away homewards,

with a quickened pace, without expectation of seeing him in a considerable while; and yet when they were got near home, to their astonishment, they found him on foot with them, having a basket of strawberries. G. B. immediately then fell to chiding his wife on the account of what she had been speaking to her brother of him on the road, which, when they wondered at, he said, he knew their thoughts.   Ruck, being startled at that, made some reply, intimating that the devil himself did not know so far; but G. B. answered, my God makes known your thoughts unto me.   The prisoner now at the bar had nothing to answer unto what was thus witnessed against him, that was worth considering.   Only he said, Ruck and his wife left a man with him when they left him, which Ruck now affirmed to be false; and when the Court asked G. B. what the man's name was his countenance was much altered, nor could he say who it was.   But the Court began to think that he then stepped aside only that by the assistance of the black man he might put on his invisibility, and in that fascinating mist gratify his own jealous humour to hear what they said of him. Which trick of rendering themselves invisible our witches do in their confessions pretend that they sometimes are masters of; and it is the more credible, because there is demonstration that they often render many other things utterly invisible.

VIII. Faltering, faulty, unconstant, and contrary answers upon judicial and deliberate examination are counted some unlucky symptoms of guilt in all crimes, especially in witchcrafts.   Now there never was a prisoner more eminent for them than G. B., both at his examination and on his trial.   His tergiversations, contradictions, and falsehoods were very sensible: he had little to say, but that he had heard some things that he could not prove, reflecting upon the reputation of some of the witnesses. Only he gave in a paper to the jury; wherein, although he had many times before granted, not only that there are witches, but also that the present sufferings of the country are the effects of horrible witchcrafts; yet he now goes to evince it, that there neither are, nor ever were, witches that, having made a compact with the devil, can send a devil to torment other people at a distance. This paper was transcribed out of Ady, which the Court presently knew, as soon as they heard it. But he said he had taken none of it out of any book, for which his evasion afterwards was, that a gentleman gave him the discourse in a manuscript, from whence he transcribed it.

IX. The jury brought him in guilty; but when he came to die he utterly denied the fact whereof he had been thus convicted.

II.

THE TRIAL OF BRIDGET BISHOP,
ALIAS OLIVER,

At the Court of Oyer and Terminer, held at Salem, June 2, 1692.

I. She was indicted for bewitching of several persons in the neighbourhood, the indictment being drawn up according to the form in such cases usual. And pleading "Not guilty," there were brought in several persons, who had long undergone many kinds of miseries, which were preternaturally inflicted, and generally ascribed unto a horrible witchcraft. There was little occasion to prove the witchcraft, it being evident and notorious to all beholders. Now to fix the witchcraft on the prisoner at the bar, the first thing used was the testimony of the bewitched, whereof several testified that the shape of the prisoner did oftentimes very grievously pinch them, choke them, bite them, and afflict them, urging them to write their names in a book which the said spectre called " ours." One of them did further testify that it was the shape of this prisoner, with another, which one day took her from her wheel, and, carrying her to the riverside, threatened there to drown her if she did not sign to the book mentioned, which yet she refused. Others of them did also testify that the said shape did in her threats brag to them that she had been the death of sundry persons, then by her named; that she had ridden a man, then likewise named. Another testified the apparition of ghosts unto the spectre of Bishop, crying out, " You murdered us!" About the truth whereof there was in the matter of fact but too much suspicion.

II. It was testified that, at the examination of the prisoner before the magistrates, the bewitched were extremely tortured. If she did but cast her eyes on them, they were presently struck down, and this in such a manner as there could be no collusion in the business. But upon the touch of her hand upon them, when they lay in their swoons, they would immediately revive, and not upon the touch of any one else. Moreover, upon some special actions of her body, as the shaking of her head, or the turning of her eyes, they presently and painfully fell into the like postures. And many of the like accidents now fell out, while she was at the bar, one at the same time testifying that she said she could not be troubled to see the afflicted thus tormented.

III. There was testimony likewise brought in, that a man striking once at the place where a bewitched person said the shape of this Bishop stood, the bewitched cried out that he had tore her coat in the place then particularly specified; and the woman's coat was found to be torn in that very place.

IV. One Deliverance Hobbs, who had confessed her being a witch, was now tormented by the spectres for her confession; and she now testified that this Bishop tempted her to sign the book again, and to deny what she had confessed. She affirmed that it was the shape of this prisoner which whipped her with iron rods to compel her thereunto; and she affirmed that this Bishop was at a general meeting of the witches in a field at Salem Village, and there partook of a diabolical sacrament in bread and wine then administered.

V. To render it further unquestionable that the prisoner at the bar was the person truly charged in this witchcraft, there were produced many evidences of other witchcrafts by her perpetrated. For instance, John Cook testified that about five or six years ago, one morning, about sunrise, he was in his chamber assaulted by the shape of this prisoner, which looked on him, grinned at him, and very much hurt him with a blow on the side of the head; and that on the same day, about noon, the same shape walked in the room where he was, and an apple strangely flew out of his hand into the lap of his mother, six or eight feet from him.

VI. Samuel Gray testified that, about fourteen years ago, he waked on a night, and saw the room

where he lay full of light; and that he then saw plainly
a woman between the cradle and the bedside, which
looked upon him. He rose and it vanished, though
he found the doors all fast. Looking out at the entry
door he saw the same woman in the same garb again,
and said, " In God's name, what do you come for?" He
went to bed, and had the same woman again assaulting
him. The child in the cradle gave a great screech,
and the woman disappeared. It was long before the
child could be quieted; and though it were a very likely
thriving child, yet from this time it pined away, and,
after divers months, died in a sad condition. He knew
not Bishop, nor her name; but when he saw her after
this he knew by her countenance, and apparel, and
all circumstances, that it was the apparition of this
Bishop which had thus troubled him.

VII. John Bly and his wife testified that he bought
a sow of Edward Bishop, the husband of the prisoner,
and was to pay the price agreed unto another person.
This prisoner, being angry that she was thus hindered
from fingering the money, quarrelled with Bly, soon
after which the sow was taken with strange fits—
jumping, leaping, and knocking her head against the
fence. She seemed blind and deaf, and would neither
eat nor be sucked. Whereupon a neighbour said she
believed the creature was overlooked; and sundry
other circumstances concurred, which made the
deponents believe that Bishop had bewitched it.

VIII. Richard Coman testified that eight years ago,
as he lay awake in his bed with a light burning in the
room, he was annoyed with the apparition of this
Bishop, and of two more that were strangers to him,
who came and oppressed him so that he could neither
stir himself nor wake any one else; and that he was

the night after molested again in the like manner, the
said Bishop taking him by the throat and pulling him
almost out of the bed.   His kinsman offered for this
cause to lodge with him; and that night, as they were
awake discoursing together, this Coman was once
more visited by the guests which had formerly been
so troublesome, his kinsman being at the same time
struck speechless, and unable to move hand or foot.
He had laid his sword by him, which these unhappy
spectres did strive much to wrest from him, only he
held too fast for them.   He then grew able to call the
people of his house; but although they heard him, yet
they had not power to speak or stir, until at last, one
of the people crying out, "What's the matter?" the
spectres all vanished.

IX. Samuel Shattock testified that, in the year 1680,
this Bridget Bishop often came to his house upon such
frivolous and foolish errands that they suspected she
came indeed with a purpose of mischief.   Presently,
whereupon, his eldest child, which was of as promising
health and sense as any child of its age, began to droop
exceedingly; and the oftener that Bishop came to the
house the worse grew the child.   As the child would
be standing at the door he would be thrown and
bruised against the stones by an invisible hand, and in
like sort knock his face against the sides of the house
and bruise it after a miserable manner.   Afterwards
this Bishop would bring him things to dye, whereof
he could not imagine any use; and when she paid him
a piece of money the purse and money were unaccountably conveyed out of a locked box, and never seen any
more.   The child was immediately hereupon taken
with terrible fits, whereof his friends thought he would
have died.   Indeed, he did almost nothing but cry and

sleep for several months together, and at length his understanding was utterly taken away. Among other symptoms of an enchantment upon him one was, that there was a board in the garden whereon he would walk, and all the invitations in the world could never fetch him off. About seventeen or eighteen years after there came a stranger to Shattock's house, who, seeing the child, said, " This poor child is bewitched; and you have a neighbour living not far off who is a witch." He added, " Your neighbour has had a falling out with your wife; and she said, in her heart, your wife is a proud woman, and she would bring down her pride in this child." He then remembered that Bishop had parted from his wife in muttering and menacing terms a little before the child was taken ill. The abovesaid stranger would needs carry the bewitched boy with him to Bishop's house on pretence of buying a pot of cyder. The woman entertained him in furious manner, and flew also upon the boy, scratching his face till the blood came, and saying, " Thou rogue, what dost thou bring this fellow here to plague me?" Now it seems the man had said, before he went, that he would fetch blood of her. Ever after the boy was followed with grievous fits, which the doctors themselves generally ascribed unto witchcraft, and wherein he would be thrown still into the fire or the water if he were not constantly looked after; and it was verily believed that Bishop was the cause of it.

X. John Louder testified that, upon some little controversy with Bishop about her fowls going well to bed, he did awake in the night by moonlight, and did see clearly the likeness of this woman grievously oppressing him, in which miserable condition she held him, unable to help himself, till near day. He told

Bishop of this; but she denied it, and threatened him
very much. Quickly after this, being at home on a
Lord's day with the doors shut about him, he saw a
black pig approach him, at which, he going to kick,
it vanished away. Immediately after, sitting down,
he saw a black thing jump in at the window, and come
and stand before him. The body was like that of a
monkey, the feet like a cock's, but the face much like a
man's. He being so extremely affrighted that he could
not speak, this monster spoke to him, and said, "I
am a messenger sent unto you, for I understand that
you are in some trouble of mind; and if you will be
ruled by me, you shall want for nothing in this world."
Whereupon he endeavoured to clap his hands upon
it, but he could feel no substance; and it jumped out
of the window again, but immediately came in by the
porch, though the doors were shut, and said, "You
had better take my counsel!" He then struck at it
with a stick, but struck only the ground-sel and broke
the stick. The arm with which he struck was presently disenabled, and it vanished away. He presently
went out at the back door and spied this Bishop, in
her orchard, going toward her house, but he had not
power to set one foot forward unto her. Whereupon,
returning into the house, he was immediately accosted
by the monster he had seen before, which goblin was
now going to fly at him, whereat he cried out, "The
whole armour of God be between me and you!" So
it sprang back, and flew over the apple-tree, shaking
many apples off the tree in its flying over. At its leap
it flung dirt with its feet against the stomach of the
man, whereon he was then struck dumb, and so continued for three days together. Upon the producing
of this testimony Bishop denied that she knew this

deponent. Yet their two orchards joined, and they had often had their little quarrels for some years together.

XI. William Stacy testified that, receiving money of this Bishop for work done by him, he was gone but a matter of three rods from her, and, looking for his money, found it unaccountably gone from him. Some time after Bishop asked him whether his father would grind her grist for her. He demanded why. She replied, "Because folks count me a witch." He answered, "No question but he will grind it for you." Being then gone about six rods from her, with a small load in his cart, suddenly the off-wheel stumped and sunk down into a hole upon plain ground, so that the deponent was forced to get help for the recovering of the wheel. But stepping back to look for the hole which might give him this disaster, there was none at all to be found. Some time after he was wakened in the night, but it seemed as light as day, and he perfectly saw the shape of this Bishop in the room troubling of him; but upon her going out all was dark again. He charged Bishop afterwards with it, and she denied it not, but was very angry. Quickly after, this deponent having been threatened by Bishop, as he was in a dark night going to the barn, he was very suddenly taken or lifted from the ground and thrown against a stone wall. After that he was again hoisted up and thrown down a bank at the end of his house. After this, again, passing by this Bishop, his horse, with a small load, striving to draw, all his gears flew to pieces, and the cart fell down; and this deponent, going then to lift a bag of corn of about two bushels, could not budge it with all his might.

Many other pranks of this Bishop's this deponent was ready to testify. He also testified that he verily believed the said Bishop was the instrument of his daughter Priscilla's death, of which suspicion pregnant reasons were assigned.

XII. To crown all, John Bly and William Bly testified that, being employed by Bridget Bishop to help to take down the cellar wall of the old house wherein she formerly lived, they did in holes of the said old wall find several poppets, made up of rags and hog's bristles, with headless pins in them, the points being outward, whereof she could give no account unto the Court that was reasonable or tolerable.

XIII. One thing that made against the prisoner was her being evidently convicted of gross lying in the Court, several times, while she was making her plea; but besides this, a jury of women found a preternatural teat upon her body. But upon a second search, within three or four hours, there was no such thing to be seen. There was also an account of other people whom this woman had afflicted; and there might have been many more if they had been enquired for, but there was no need of them.

XIV. There was one very strange thing more with which the Court was newly entertained. As this woman was under a guard passing by the great and spacious meeting house of Salem, she gave a look towards the house, and immediately a demon, invisibly entering the meeting house, tore down a part of it, so that, though there was no person to be seen there, yet the people, at the noise, running in, found a board, which was strongly fastened with several nails, transported unto another quarter of the house.

III.

THE TRIAL OF SUSANNA MARTIN,

At the Court of Oyer and Terminer, held by
Adjournment at Salem, June 29, 1692.

I. Susanna Martin, pleading "Not guilty" to the
indictment of witchcraft brought in against her, there
were produced the evidences of many persons very
sensibly and grievously bewitched, who all complained
of the prisoner at the bar as the person whom they
believed the cause of their miseries. And now, as
well as in the other trials, there was an extraordinary
endeavour by witchcrafts, with cruel and frequent fits,
to hinder the poor sufferers from giving in their complaints, which the Court was forced with much
patience to obtain, by much waiting and watching
for it.

II. There was now also an account given of what
passed at her first examination before the magistrates.
The cast of her eye, then striking the afflicted people
to the ground, whether they saw that cast or no; there
were these among other passages between the magistrates and the examinate.

Magistrate: Pray, what ails these people?

Martin: I don't know.

Magistrate: But what do you think ails them?

Martin: I don't desire to spend my judgment
upon it.

Magistrate: Don't you think they are bewitched?

Martin: No, I do not think they are.

Magistrate: Tell us your thoughts about them then.

Martin: No, my thoughts are my own, when they are in, but when they are out they are another's. Their master——

Magistrate: Their master? Who do you think is their master?

Martin: If they be dealing in the black art, you may know as well as I.

Magistrate: Well, what have you done towards this?

Martin: Nothing at all.

Magistrate: Why, it is you or your appearance.

Martin: I cannot help it.

Magistrate: Is it not your master? How comes your appearance to hurt these?

Martin: How do I know? He that appeared in the shape of Samuel, a glorified saint, may appear in any one's shape.

It was then also noted in her, as in others like her, that if the afflicted went to approach her they were flung down to the ground. And when she was asked the reason of it she said, "I cannot tell; it may be the devil bears me more malice than another."

III. The Court accounted themselves alarumed by these things to enquire further into the conversation of the prisoner, and see what there might occur to render these accusations further credible. Whereupon John Allen, of Salisbury, testified that, he refusing, because of the weakness of his oxen, to cart some staves at the request of this Martin, she was displeased at it, and said, "It had been as good that he had, for his oxen should never do him much more service." Whereupon this deponent said, "Dost thou threaten me, thou old witch? I'll throw thee into the brook," which to avoid she flew over the bridge and escaped. But, as he was going home, one of his oxen tired, so that he was forced to unyoke him that he might get him home. He then put his oxen, with many more, upon Salisbury Beach, where cattle did use to get flesh. In a few days all the oxen upon the beach were found by their tracks to have run unto the mouth of Merrimack River, and not returned; but the next day they were found come ashore upon Plum Island. They that sought them used all imaginable gentleness, but they would still run away with a violence that seemed wholly diabolical till they came near the mouth of Merrimack River, when they ran right into the sea, swimming as far as they could be seen. One of them then swam back again with a swiftness amazing to the beholders, who stood ready to receive him, and help up his tired carcass; but the beast ran furiously up into the island, and from thence through the marshes up into Newbury Town, and so up into the woods, and there, after a while, found near Amesbury. So that of fourteen good oxen there was only this saved. The rest were all cast up, some in one place, and some in another, drowned.

IV. John Atkinson testified that he exchanged a cow with a son of Susanna Martin's, whereat she muttered, and was unwilling he should have it. Going to receive this cow, though he hamstringed her and haltered her, she, of a tame creature, grew so mad that they could scarce get her along. She broke all the ropes that were fastened unto her, and though she was tied fast unto a tree, yet she made her escape and gave them such further trouble as they could ascribe to no cause but witchcraft.

V. Bernard Peache testified that, being in bed on the Lord's-day night, he heard a scrabbling at the window, whereat he then saw Susanna Martin come in and jump down upon the floor. She took hold of this deponent's feet, and drawing his body up into a heap, she lay upon him near two hours, in all which time he could neither speak nor stir. At length, when he could begin to move, he laid hold on her hand, and, pulling it up to his mouth, he bit three of her fingers, as he judged, unto the bone. Whereupon she went from the chamber, down the stairs, out at the door. This deponent thereupon called unto the people of the house to advise them of what passed, and he himself did follow her. The people saw her not; but there being a bucket at the left hand of the door, there was a drop of blood found upon it, and several more drops of blood upon the snow newly fallen abroad. There was likewise the print of her two feet just without the threshold, but no more sign of any footing further off.

At another time this deponent was desired by the prisoner to come unto an husking of corn at her house, and she said, "If he did not come, it were better that he did!" He went not; but the night following Susanna Martin, as he judged, and another came towards him. One of them said, "Here he is!" But he, having a quarter-staff, made a blow at them. The roof of the barn broke his blow, but, following them to the window, he made another blow at them, and struck them down; yet they got up, and got out, and he saw no more of them.

About this time there was a rumour about the town that Martin had a broken head, but the deponent could say nothing to that.

The said Peache also testified the bewitching the cattle to death upon Martin's discontents.

VI. Robert Downer testified that this prisoner, being some years ago prosecuted at Court for a witch, he then said unto her he believed she was a witch. Whereat she, being dissatisfied, said that some she-devil would shortly fetch him away, which words were heard by others, as well as himself. The night following, as he lay in his bed, there came in at the window the likeness of a cat, which flew upon him, took fast hold of his throat, lay on him a considerable while, and almost killed him. At length he remembered what Susanna Martin had threatened the day before, and with much striving he cried out, " Avoid, thou she-devil! In the name of God the Father, the Son, and the Holy Ghost, avoid!" Whereupon it left him, leaped on the floor, and flew out at the window.

And there also came in several testimonies that before ever Downer spoke a word of this accident Susanna Martin and her family had related how this Downer had been handled!

VII. John Kembal testified that Susanna Martin, upon a causeless disgust, had threatened him about a certain cow of his, that she should never do him any more good, and it came to pass accordingly. For soon after the cow was found stark dead on the dry ground, without any distemper to be discerned upon her. Upon which he was followed with a strange death upon more of his cattle, whereof he lost in one spring to the value of thirty pounds. But the said John Kembal had a further testimony to give in against the prisoner which was truly admirable.

Being desirous to furnish himself with a dog, he applied himself to buy one of this Martin, who had a bitch with whelps in her house. But she not letting him have his choice, he said he would supply himself

then at one Blezdels. Having marked a puppy which
he liked at Blezdels, he met George Martin, the
husband of the prisoner, going by, who asked him
whether he would not have one of his wife's puppies,
and he answered, " No." The same day one Edmond
Eliot, being at Martin's house, heard George Martin
relate where this Kembal had been and what he had
said. Whereupon Susanna Martin replied, " If I live,
I'll give him puppies enough!" Within a few days
after, this Kembal, coming out of the woods, there
arose a little black cloud in the north-west, and Kembal
immediately felt a force upon him, which made him
not able to avoid running upon the stumps of trees
that were before him, albeit he had a broad plain
cartway before him; but though he had his axe also
on his shoulder to endanger him in his falls, he could
not forbear going out of his way to tumble over them.
When he came below the meeting-house there
appeared unto him a little thing like a puppy, of a
darkish colour, and it shot backwards and forwards
between his legs. He had the courage to use all
possible endeavours of cutting it with his axe, but he
could not hit it; the puppy gave a jump from him,
and went, as to him it seemed, into the ground. Going
a little further, there appeared unto him a black puppy,
somewhat bigger than the first, but as black as a coal.
Its motions were quicker than those of his axe; it
flew at his belly and away; then at his throat; so, over
his shoulder one way, and then over his shoulder
another way. His heart now began to fail him, and
he thought the dog would have tore his throat out.
But he recovered himself, and called upon God in his
distress; and, naming the name of Jesus Christ, it
vanished away at once. The deponent spoke not one

word of these accidents for fear of affrighting his
wife. But the next morning, Edmond Eliot, going
into Martin's house, this woman asked him where
Kembal was. He replied, "At home, abed, for
ought he knew." She returned, "They say he was
frighted last night." Eliot asked, "With what?" She
answered, "With puppies." Eliot asked where she
heard of it, for he had heard nothing of it. She
rejoined, "About the town," although Kembal had
mentioned the matter to no creature living.

VIII. William Brown testified that heaven, having
blessed him with a most pious and prudent wife, this
wife of his one day met with Susanna Martin; but
when she approached just unto her Martin vanished
out of sight, and left her extremely affrighted. After
which time the said Martin often appeared unto her,
giving her no little trouble; and when she did come
she was visited with birds that sorely pecked and
pricked her; and sometimes a bunch, like a pullet's
egg, would rise in her throat, ready to choke her, till
she cried out, "Witch, you shan't choke me!" While
this good woman was in this extremity the Church
appointed a day of prayer on her behalf, whereupon
her trouble ceased; she saw not Martin as formerly,
and the Church, instead of their fast, gave thanks for
her deliverance. But a considerable while after, she
being summoned to give in some evidence at the Court
against this Martin, quickly thereupon, this Martin
came behind her while she was milking her cow, and
said unto her, "For thy defaming her at Court, I'll
make thee the miserablest creature in the world."
Soon after which she fell into a strange kind of
distemper, and became horribly frantic, and incapable
of any reasonable action, the physicians declaring that

her distemper was preternatural, and that some devil had certainly bewitched her; and in that condition she now remained.

IX. Sarah Atkinson testified that Susanna Martin came from Amesbury to their house at Newbury in an extraordinary season, when it was not fit for any to travel. She came (as she said unto Atkinson) all that long way on foot. She bragged and shewed how dry she was; nor could it be perceived that so much as the soles of her shoes were wet. Atkinson was amazed at it, and professed that she should herself have been wet up to the knees if she had then come so far; but Martin replied, " She scorned to be drabbled!" It was noted that this testimony upon her trial cast her in a very singular confusion.

X. John Pressy testified that, being one evening very unaccountably bewildered near a field of Martin's, and several times, as one under an enchantment, returning to the place he had left, at length he saw a marvellous light, about the bigness of a half-bushel, near two rod, out of the way. He went and struck at it with a stick, and laid it on with all his might. He gave it near forty blows, and felt it a palpable substance. But going from it his heels were struck up, and he was laid with his back on the ground, sliding, as he thought, into a pit, from whence he recovered by taking hold on the bush, although after-wards he could find no such pit in the place. Having, after his recovery, gone five or six rod, he saw Susanna Martin standing on his left hand, as the light had done before, but they changed no words with one another. He could scarce find his house in his return; but at length he got home extremely affrighted. The next day it was, upon enquiry, understood that Martin was in a miserable condition by pains and hurts that were upon her.

It was further testified by this deponent that after he had given in some evidence against Susanna Martin, many years ago, she gave him foul words about it; and said, " He should never prosper more "; particularly, " That he should never have more than two cows; that though he was never so likely to have more, yet he should never have them." And that from that very day to this—namely, for twenty years together, he could never exceed that number; but some strange thing or other still prevented his having any more.

XI. Jervis Ring testified that about seven years ago he was oftentimes and grievously oppressed in the night, but saw not who troubled him; until at last he, lying perfectly awake, plainly saw Susanna Martin approach him. She came to him, and forcibly bit him by the finger, so that the print of the bite is now, so long after, to be seen upon him.

XII. But besides all of these evidences, there was a most wonderful account of one Joseph Ring produced on this occasion.

This man has been strangely carried about by demons, from one witch-meeting to another, for near two years together; and for one quarter of this time they have made him and keep him dumb, though he is now again able to speak. There was one T. H., who, having, as it is judged, a design of engaging this Joseph Ring in a snare of devilism, contrived a while to bring this Ring two shillings in debt unto him.

Afterwards this poor man would be visited with unknown shapes, and this T. H. sometimes among them, which would force him away with them unto unknown places, where he saw meetings, feastings, dancings; and after his return, wherein they hurried him along through the air, he gave demonstrations to the neighbours that he had indeed been so transported. When he was brought unto these hellish meetings one of the first things they still did unto him was to give him a knock on the back, whereupon he was ever as if bound with chains, incapable of stirring out of the place till they should release him. He related that there often came to him a man who presented him a book, whereto he would have him set his hand, promising to him that he should then have even what he would, and presenting him with all the delectable things, persons, and places that he could imagine. But he, refusing to subscribe, the business would end with dreadful shapes, noises and screeches, which almost scared him out of his wits. Once with the book there was a pen offered him, and an inkhorn with liquor in it that seemed like blood; but he never touched it.

This man did now affirm that he saw the prisoner at several of those hellish rendezvous.

Note, this woman was one of the most impudent, scurrilous, wicked creatures in the world, and she did now throughout her whole trial discover herself to be such an one. Yet when she was asked what she had to say for herself, her chief plea was, "That she had led a most virtuous and holy life."

IV.

THE TRIAL OF ELIZABETH HOW,

At the Court of Oyer and Terminer, held by
Adjournment at Salem, June 30, 1692.

I. Elizabeth How, pleading " Not guilty " to the
indictment of witchcrafts, then charged upon her, the
Court, according to the usual proceedings of the
Courts in England in such cases, began with hearing
the depositions of several afflicted people, who were
grievously tortured by sensible and evident witchcrafts, and all complained of the prisoner as the cause
of their trouble. It was also found that the sufferers
were not able to bear her look, as likewise, that in
their greatest swoons, they distinguished her touch
from other people's, being thereby raised out of them.

And there was other testimony of people to whom
the shape of this How gave trouble nine or ten years
ago.

II. It has been a most usual thing for the
bewitched persons, at the same time that the spectres
representing the witches troubled them, to be visited
with apparitions of ghosts, pretending to have been
murdered by the witches then represented. And
sometimes the confessions of the witches afterwards
acknowledged those very murders which these apparitions charged upon them, although they had never
heard what informations had been given by the
sufferers.

There were such apparitions of ghosts testified by
some of the present sufferers; and the ghosts affirmed

that this How had murdered them : which things were feared, but not proved.

III. This How had made some attempts of joining to the Church at Ipswich several years ago, but she was denied an admission into that holy society, partly through a suspicion of witchcraft then urged against her. And there now came in testimony of preternatural mischiefs, presently befalling some that had been instrumental to debar her from the communion whereupon she was intruding.

IV. There was a particular deposition of Joseph Stafford, that his wife had conceived an extreme aversion to this How, on the reports of her witchcrafts; but How one day, taking her by the hand, and saying, "I believe you are not ignorant of the great scandal that I lie under, by an evil report raised upon me," she immediately, unreasonably and unpersuadeably, even like one enchanted, began to take this woman's part. How being soon after propounded, as desiring an admission to the Table of the Lord, some of the pious brethren were unsatisfied about her. The elders appointed a meeting to hear matters objected against her; and no arguments in the world could hinder this good wife Stafford from going to the lecture. She did indeed promise, with much ado, that she would not go to the Church-meeting, yet she could not refrain going thither also. How's affairs there were so canvassed that she came off rather guilty than cleared; nevertheless good wife Stafford could not forbear taking her by the hand, and saying, "Though you are condemned before men, you are justified before God." She was quickly taken in a very strange manner, ranting, raving, raging, and crying out, "Goody How must come into the Church; she is a precious saint; and though she be condemned before men, she is justified before God." So she continued for the space of two or three hours, and then fell into a trance; but coming to herself, she cried out, " Ha! I was mistaken," and afterwards again repeated, " Ha! I was mistaken! " Being asked by a stander-by, "Wherein?" she replied, "I thought Goody How had been a precious saint of God, but now I see she is a witch. She has bewitched me, and my child, and we shall never be well till there be a testimony for her that she may be taken into the Church." And How said afterwards that she was very sorry to see Stafford at the Church-meeting mentioned. Stafford, after this, declared herself to be afflicted by the shape of How; and from that shape she endured many miseries.

V. John How, brother to the husband of the prisoner, testified that he, refusing to accompany the prisoner unto her examination, as was by her desired, immediately some of his cattle were bewitched to death, leaping three or four feet high, turning about, speaking, falling, and dying at once; and going to cut off an ear, for a use that might as well perhaps have been omitted, the hand wherein he held his knife was taken very numb, and so it remained, and full of pain, for several days, being not well at this very time. And he suspected the prisoner for the author of it.

VI. Nehemiah Abbot testified that unusual and mischievous accidents would befall his cattle whenever he had any difference with this prisoner. Once, particularly, she wished his ox choked, and within a little while that ox was choked with a turnip in his throat. At another time, refusing to lend his horse at the request of her daughter, the horse was in a preternatural manner abused.   And several other odd things of that kind were testified.

VII. There came in testimony that one good wife Sherwin, upon some difference with How, was bewitched, and that she died, charging this How with having a hand in her death; and that other people had their barrels of drink unaccountably mischieved, spoiled, and spilt upon their displeasing of her.

The things in themselves were trivial, but there being such a course of them it made them the more considered. Among others, Martha Wood gave her testimony that a little after her father had been employed in gathering an account of How's conversation they once and again lost great quantities of drink out of their vessels, in such a manner as they could ascribe to nothing but witchcraft; as also that How, giving her some apples, when she had eaten of them she was taken with a very strange kind of amaze, insomuch that she knew not what she said or did.

VIII. There was likewise a cluster of depositions that one Isaac Cummings, refusing to lend his mare unto the husband of this How, the mare was within a day or two taken in a strange condition; the beast seemed much abused, being bruised as if she had been running over the rocks, and marked where the bridle went, as if burnt with a red-hot bridle. Moreover, one using a pipe of tobacco for the cure of the beast, a blue flame issued out of her, took hold of her hair, and not only spread and burnt on her, but it also flew upwards towards the roof of the barn, and had like to have set the barn on fire; and the mare died very suddenly.

IX. Timothy Pearly and his wife testified not only unaccountable mischiefs befell their cattle upon their having of differences with this prisoner; but also that they had a daughter destroyed by witchcrafts, which daughter still charged How as the cause of her affliction; and it was noted that she would be struck down whenever How was spoken of. She was often endeavoured to be thrown into the fire, and into the water, in her strange fits. Though her father had corrected her for charging How with bewitching her, yet (as was testified by others also) she said, "She was sure of it, and must die standing to it." Accordingly she charged How to the very death, and said, "Though How could afflict and torment her body, yet she could not hurt her soul," and "That the truth of this matter would appear when she would be dead and gone."

X. Francis Lane testified that, being hired by the husband of this How to get him a parcel of posts and rails, this Lane hired John Pearly to assist him. This prisoner then told Lane that she believed the posts and rails would not do, because John Pearly helped him; but that if he had got them alone, without John Pearly's help, they might have done well enough. When James How came to receive his posts and rails of Lane, How taking them up by the ends, they, though good and sound, yet unaccountably broke off, so that Lane was forced to get thirty or forty more; and this prisoner being informed of it, she said, "She told him so before, because Pearly helped about them."

XI. Afterwards there came in the confessions of several other (penitent) witches, which affirmed this How to be one of those who, with them, had been baptized by the devil in the river at Newbury Falls, before which he made them there kneel down by the brink of the river and worship him.

V.

THE TRIAL OF MARTHA CARRIER,

At the Court of Oyer and Terminer, held by
Adjournment at Salem, August 2, 1692.

I. Martha Carrier was indicted for the bewitching
certain persons, according to the form usual in such
cases, pleading " Not guilty " to her indictment.   There
were first brought in a considerable number of the
bewitched persons, who not only made the Court
sensible of an horrid witchcraft committed upon them,
but also deposed that it was Martha Carrier, or her
shape, that grievously tormented them, by biting,
pricking, pinching, and choking of them.   It was
further deposed that while this Carrier was on her
examination before the magistrates the poor people
were so tortured that every one expected their death
upon the very spot, but that upon the binding of
Carrier they were eased.   Moreover, the look of
Carrier then laid the afflicted people for dead; and her
touch, if her eye at the same time were off them, raised
them again; which things were also now seen upon
her trial.   And it was testified that upon the mention
of some having their necks twisted almost round, by
the shape of this Carrier, she replied, " It is no matter
though their necks had been twisted quite off."

II. Before the trial of this prisoner several of her
own children had frankly and fully confessed not only
that they were witches themselves, but that this their
mother had made them so.   This confession they made
with great shows of repentance and with much demonstration of truth.   They related place, time, occasion;

12

they gave an account of journeys, meetings, and mischiefs by them performed, and were very credible in what they said.   Nevertheless, this evidence was not produced against the prisoner at the bar, inasmuch as there was other evidence enough to proceed upon.

III. Benjamin Abbot gave his testimony that last March was a twelvemonth, this Carrier was very angry with him upon laying out some land near her husband's.   Her expressions in this anger were, " That she would stick as close to Abbot as the bark stuck to the tree; and that he should repent of it afore seven years came to an end, so as Doctor Prescot should never cure him."   These words were heard by others besides Abbot himself, who also heard her say, " She would hold his nose as close to the grindstone as ever it was held since his name was Abbot."   Presently, after this, he was taken with a swelling in his foot and then with a pain in his side, and exceedingly tormented. It bred into a sore, which was lanced by Doctor Prescot, and several gallons of corruption ran out of it.   For six weeks it continued very bad, and then another sore bred in the groin, which was also lanced by Doctor Prescot.   Another sore then bred in his groin, which was likewise cut, and put him to very great misery.   He was brought unto death's door, and so remained until Carrier was taken and carried away by the constable, from which very day he began to mend, and so grew better every day, and is well ever since.

Sarah Abbot also, his wife, testified that her husband was not only all this while afflicted in his body, but also that strange, extraordinary, and unaccountable calamities befell his cattle, their death being such as they could guess at no natural reason for.

IV. Allin Toothaker testified that Richard, the son of Martha Carrier, having some difference with him, pulled him down by the hair of the head. When he rose again he was going to strike at Richard Carrier, but fell down flat on his back to the ground, and had not power to stir hand or foot until he told Carrier he yielded, and then he saw the shape of Martha Carrier go off his breast.

This Toothaker had received a wound in the wars, and he now testified that Martha Carrier told him " He should never be cured." Just afore the apprehending of Carrier he could thrust a knitting-needle into his wound four inches deep, but presently, after her being seized, he was thoroughly healed.

He further testified that when Carrier and he sometimes were at variance she would clap her hands at him, and say, " He should get nothing by it," whereupon he several times lost his cattle by strange deaths, whereof no natural causes could be given.

V. John Rogger also testified that upon the threatening words of this malicious Carrier his cattle would be strangely bewitched; as was more particularly then described.

VI. Samuel Preston testified that about two years ago, having some difference with Martha Carrier, he lost a cow in a strange, preternatural, unusual manner; and about a month after this the said Carrier, having again some difference with him, she told him " He had lately lost a cow, and it should not be long before he lost another," which accordingly came to pass, for he had a thriving and well-kept cow which, without any known cause, quickly fell down and died.

VII. Phebe Chandler testified that about a fortnight before the apprehension of Martha Carrier, on a Lord's-day, while the Psalm was singing in the church, this Carrier then took her by the shoulder and, shaking her, asked her "Where she lived"; she made her no answer, although as Carrier, who lived next door to her father's house, could not in reason but know who she was. Quickly after this, as she was at several times crossing the fields, she heard a voice, that she took to be Martha Carrier's, and it seemed as if it was over her head. The voice told her " She should within two or three days be poisoned." Accordingly, within such a little time, one half of her right hand became greatly swollen and very painful, as also part of her face, whereof she can give no account how it came. It continued very bad for some days, and several times since she has had a great pain in her breast, and been so seized on her legs that she has hardly been able to go. She added that lately, going well to the House of God, Richard, the son of Martha Carrier, looked very earnestly upon her, and immediately her hand, which had formerly been poisoned, as is above said, began to pain her greatly, and she had a strange burning at her stomach; but was then struck deaf, so that she could not hear any of the prayer, or singing, till the two or three last words of the Psalm.

VIII. One Foster, who confessed her own share in the witchcraft for which the prisoner stood indicted, affirmed that she had seen the prisoner at some of their witch-meetings, and that it was this Carrier who persuaded her to be a witch. She confessed that the devil carried them on a pole to a witch-meeting, but the pole broke, and she, hanging about Carrier's neck, they both fell down, and she then received a hurt by the fall, whereof she was not at this very time recovered.

IX. One Lacy, who likewise confessed her share in this witchcraft, now testified that she and the prisoner were once bodily present at a witch-meeting in Salem village; and that she knew the prisoner to be a witch, and to have been at a diabolical sacrament, and that the prisoner was the undoing of her, and her children, by enticing them into the snare of the devil.

X. Another Lacy, who also confessed her share in this witchcraft, now testified that the prisoner was at the witch-meeting in Salem village, where they had bread and wine administered unto them.

XI. In the time of this prisoner's trial one Susanna Sheldon, in open Court, had her hands unaccountably tied together with a wheel-band, so fast that without cutting it could not be loosed. It was done by a spectre; and the sufferer affirmed it was the prisoner's.

Memorandum: This rampant hag, Martha Carrier, was the person of whom the confessions of the witches, and of her own children among the rest, agreed that the devil had promised her she should be Queen of Heb.

A FURTHER

ACCOUNT OF THE TRIALS

OF THE

New England Witches

A True Narrative of some Remarkable Passages
relating to sundry Persons afflicted by Witchcraft
at Salem Village in New England, which happened
from the 19th of March to the 5th of April, 1692.

Collected by Deodat Lawson.

On the nineteenth day of March last I went to
Salem Village, and lodged at Nathaniel Ingersol's,
near to the minister, Mr. P.'s house, and presently,
after I came into my lodging, Captain Walcut's
daughter Mary came to Lieut. Ingersol's and spoke to
me; but suddenly after, as she stood by the door, was
bitten, so that she cried out of her wrist, and looking
on it with a candle we saw apparently the marks of
teeth, both upper and lower set, on each side of her
wrist.

In the beginning of the evening I went to give Mr. P.
a visit. When I was there his kinswoman, Abigail
Williams (about twelve years of age), had a grievous
fit; she was at first hurried with violence to and fro in

the room (though Mrs. Ingersol endeavoured to hold her), sometimes making as if she would fly, stretching up her arms as high as she could, and crying, " Whish, whish, whish," several times; presently after she said there was Goodw. N. and said, " Do you not see her? Why there she stands! " And she said Goodw. N. offered her the book, but she was resolved she would not take it, saying often, " I won't, I won't, I won't take it. I do not know what book it is; I am sure it is none of God's book; it is the devil's book for ought I know." After that she ran to the fire, and began to throw firebrands about the house, and run against the back, as if she would run up the chimney, and, as they said, she had attempted to go into the fire in other fits.

On Lord's-day, the twentieth of March, there were sundry of the afflicted persons at meeting, as Mrs. Pope, and Goodwife Bibber, Abigail Williams, Mary Walcut, Mary Lewes, and Doctor Griggs's maid. There was also at meeting Goodwife C. (who was afterwards examined on suspicion of being a witch). They had several sore fits in the time of public worship, which did something interrupt me in my first prayer, being so unusual. After Psalm was sung, Abigail Williams said to me, " Now stand up, and name your text! " And after it was read she said, " It is a long text." In the beginning of the sermon Mrs. Pope, a woman afflicted, said to me, " Now there is enough of that." And in the afternoon Abigail Williams, upon my referring to my doctrine, said to me, " I know no doctrine you had. If you did name one, I have forgot it."

In sermon-time, when Goodwife C. was present in the meeting-house, Ab. W. called out, " Look where

Goodwife C. sits on the beam sucking her yellow bird betwixt her fingers!" Ann Putman, another girl afflicted, said, "There was a yellow bird sat on my hat as it hung on the pin in the pulpit"; but those that were by restrained her from speaking aloud about it.

On Monday, the 21st of March, the magistrates of Salem appointed to come to examination of Goodwife C., and about twelve of the clock they went into the meeting-house, which was thronged with spectators. Mr. Noyes began with a very pertinent and pathetical prayer; and Goodwife C., being called to answer to what was alleged against her, she desired to go to prayer, which was much wondered at, in the presence of so many hundred people. The magistrates told her they would not admit it; they came not there to hear her pray, but to examine her in what was alleged against her. The worshipful Mr. Hathorne asked her, "Why she afflicted those children?" She said she did not afflict them. He asked her who did then? She said, "I do not know. How should I know?" The number of the afflicted persons were about that time ten—viz. four married women, Mrs. Pope, Mrs. Putman, Goodwife Bibber, and an ancient woman named Goodall; three maids, Mary Walcut, Mercy Lewis at Thomas Putman's, and a maid at Dr. Griggs's; there were three girls from nine to twelve years of age, each of them, or thereabouts— viz. Elizabeth Parris, Abigail Williams, and Ann Putman. These were most of them at Goodwife C.'s examination, and did vehemently accuse her in the assembly of afflicting them, by biting, pinching, strangling, &c., and that they in their fits see her likeness coming to them, and bringing a book to them.

She said she had no book; they affirmed she had a
yellow bird, that used to suck betwixt her fingers,
and being asked about it, if she had any familiar spirit
that attended her, she said, " She had no familiarity
with any such thing. She was a Gospel woman ";
which title she called herself by; and the afflicted
persons told her, " Ah! she was a Gospel witch."
Ann Putman did there affirm that one day, when
Lieutenant Fuller was at prayer at her father's house,
she saw the shape of Goodwife C., and she thought
Goodwife N. praying at the same time to the devil.
She was not sure it was Goodwife N.; she thought it
was; but very sure she saw the shape of Goodwife C.
The said C. said they were poor distracted children,
and no heed to be given to what they said.   Mr.
Hathorne and Mr. Noyes replied it was the judgment
of all that were present they were bewitched, and
only she, the accused person, said they were distracted.   It was observed several times that if she did
but bite her underlip in time of examination the
persons afflicted were bitten on their arms and wrists,
and produced the marks before the magistrates,
ministers, and others; and being watched for that, if
she did but pinch her fingers or grasp one hand hard
in another, they were pinched and produced the marks
before the magistrates and spectators.   After that it
was observed that if she did but lean her breast against
the seat in the meeting-house (being the bar at which
she stood), they were afflicted.   Particularly Mrs.
Pope complained of grievous torment in her bowels,
as if they were torn out.   She vehemently accused the
said C. as the instrument, and first threw her muff at
her; but that flying not home, she got off her shoe, and
hit Goodwife C. on the head with it.   After these

postures were watched, if the said C. did but stir her feet they were afflicted in their feet, and stamped fearfully. The afflicted persons asked her why she did not go to the company of witches which were before the meeting-house mustering. Did she not hear the drum beat? They accused her of having familiarity with the devil, in the time of examination, in the shape of a black man whispering in her ear; they affirmed that her yellow bird sucked betwixt her fingers in the assembly; and order being given to see if there were any sign, the girl that saw it said it was too late now; she had removed a pin and put it on her head, which was found there sticking upright.

They told her she had covenanted with the devil for ten years; six of them were gone, and four more to come. She was required by the magistrates to answer that question in the Catechism, "How many persons be there in the Godhead?" She answered it but oddly, yet was there no great thing to be gathered from it; she denied all that was charged upon her, and said, "They could not prove a witch." She was that afternoon committed to Salem Prison, and after she was in custody she did not so appear to them and afflict them as before.

On Wednesday, the 23rd of March, I went to Thomas Putman's on purpose to see his wife. I found her lying on the bed, having had a sore fit a little before. She spoke to me, and said she was glad to see me. Her husband and she both desired me to pray with her while she was sensible, which I did, though the apparition said, "I should not go to prayer." At the first beginning she attended; but after a little time was taken with a fit, yet continued silent, and seemed to be asleep. When prayer was done, her husband,

going to her, found her in a fit; he took her off the
bed to set her on his knees, but at first she was so stiff
she could not be bended; but she afterwards sat down,
but quickly began to strive violently with her arms and
legs.   She then began to complain of, and as it were
to converse personally with, Goodwife N., saying,
"Goodwife N., be gone! Be gone! Be gone! Are
you not ashamed, a woman of your profession, to
afflict a poor creature so? What hurt did I ever do
you in my life? You have but two years to live, and
then the devil will torment your soul; for this your
name is blotted out of God's book, and it shall never
be put in God's book again. Be gone for shame; are
you not afraid of that which is coming upon you? I
know, I know what will make you afraid; the wrath
of an angry God; I am sure that will make you afraid.
Be gone, do not torment me; I know what you would
have (we judged she meant her soul), but it is out
of your reach; it is clothed with the white robes of
Christ's righteousness."   After this she seemed to
dispute with the apparition about a particular text of
Scripture.   The apparition seemed to deny it (the
woman's eyes being fast closed all this time); she said,
"She was sure there was such a text," and she would
tell it, and then the shape would be gone, for said she,
"I am sure you cannot stand before that text!"   Then
she was sorely afflicted, her mouth drawn on one side,
and her body strained for about a minute, and then
said, "I will tell, I will tell; it is, it is, it is," three or
four times, and then was afflicted to hinder her from
telling.   At last she broke forth, and said, "It is the
third chapter of the Revelations."   I did something
scruple the reading it, and did let my scruple appear,
lest Satan should make any superstitiously to improve

the Word of the Eternal God. However, though not versed in these things, I judged I might do it this once for an experiment. I began to read, and before I had near read through the first verse she opened her eyes, and was well; this fit continued near half an hour. Her husband and the spectators told me she had often been so relieved by reading texts that she named, something pertinent to her case, as Isa. xl. 1, Isa. xlix. 1, Isa. l. 1, and several others.

On Thursday, the twenty-fourth of March (being in course the lecture-day at the village), Goodwife N. was brought before the magistrates, Mr. Hathorne and Mr. Corwin, about ten of the clock in the forenoon, to be examined in the meeting-house. The Rev. Mr. Hale began with prayer, and the warrant being read, she was required to give answer "Why she afflicted those persons?" She pleaded her own innocency with earnestness. Thomas Putman's wife, Abigail Williams, and Thomas Putman's daughter accused her that she appeared to them and afflicted them in their fits; but some of the others said that they had seen her, but knew not that ever she had hurt them; amongst which was Mary Walcut, who was presently after she had so declared bitten and cried out of her in the meeting-house, producing the marks of teeth on her wrist. It was so disposed that I had not leisure to attend the whole time of examination, but both magistrates and ministers told me that the things alleged by the afflicted, and defences made by her, were much after the same manner as the former was. And her motions did produce like effects, as to biting, pinching, bruising, tormenting at their breasts by her leaning, and when bended back were as if their backs were broken. The afflicted persons said the black man whispered to her

in the assembly, and therefore she could not hear what
the magistrates said unto her. They also said that she
did then ride by the meeting-house, behind the black
man. Thomas Putman's wife had a grievous fit in the
time of examination, to the very great impairing of
her strength, and wasting of her spirits, insomuch as
she could hardly move hand or foot when she was
carried out. Others also were there grievously
afflicted, so that there was once such a hideous screech
and noise (which I heard as I walked at a little distance
from the meeting-house) as did amaze me, and some
that were within told me the whole assembly was
struck with consternation, and they were afraid that
those that sat next to them were under the influence
of witchcraft. This woman also was that day
committed to Salem Prison. The magistrates and
ministers also did inform me that they apprehended a
child of Sarah G. and examined it, being between four
and five years of age. And as to matter of fact, they
did unanimously affirm that when this child did but
cast its eye upon the afflicted persons they were
tormented; and they held her head, and yet so many
as her eye could fix upon were afflicted, which they
did several times make careful observation of. The
afflicted complained they had often been bitten by this
child, and produced the marks of a small set of teeth
accordingly. This was also committed to Salem
Prison; the child looked hale and well as other
children. I saw it at Lieut. Ingersol's. After the
commitment of Goodwife N. Thomas Putman's wife
was much better, and had no violent fits at all from
that 24th of March to the 5th of April. Some others
also said they had not seen her so frequently appear
to them, to hurt them.

On the 25th of March (as Captain Stephen Sewal, of Salem, did afterwards inform me) Eliz. Parris had sore fits at his house, which much troubled himself and his wife, so, as he told me, they were almost discouraged. She related that the great black man came to her, and told her if she would be ruled by him she should have whatsoever she desired, and go to a golden city. She relating this to Mrs. Sewal, she told the child it was the devil, and he was a liar from the beginning, and bid her tell him so if he came again, which she did accordingly at the next coming to her in her fits.

On the 26th of March Mr. Hathorne, Mr. Corwin, and Mr. Higison were at the prison-keeper's house to examine the child, and it told them there it had a little snake that used to suck on the lowest joint of its forefinger; and when they enquired where, pointing to other places, it told them not there, but there, pointing on the lowest joint of the forefinger, where they observed a deep red spot, about the bigness of a flea-bite. They asked who gave it that snake; whether the great black man? It said no; its mother gave it.

The 31st of March there was a public fast kept at Salem on account of these afflicted persons, and Abigail Williams said that the witches had a sacrament that day at a house in the village, and that they had red bread and red drink. The first of April, Mercy Lewis, Thomas Putman's maid, in her fit, said they did eat red bread, like man's flesh, and would have had her eat some, but she would not; but turned away her head and spit at them, and said, "I will not eat, I will not drink; it is blood," &c. She said, "That is not the bread of life; that is not the water of life; Christ gives the bread of life; I will have none of it!"

The first of April also Mercy Lewis aforesaid saw in her fit a white man, and was with him in a glorious place, which had no candles nor sun, yet was full of light and brightness, where was a great multitude in white glittering robes, and they sung the song in the fifth of Revelation, the 9th verse, and the 110th Psalm and the 149th Psalm; and said with herself, " How long shall I stay here! Let me be along with you!" She was loth to leave this place, and grieved that she could tarry no longer. This white man hath appeared several times to some of them, and given them notice how long it should be before they had another fit, which was sometimes a day, or day and half, or more or less, it hath fallen out accordingly.

The 3rd of April, the Lord's-day, being Sacrament day at the village, Goodwife C., upon Mr. Parris's naming his text, John vi. 70, " One of them is a devil," the said Goodwife C. went immediately out of the meeting-house, and flung the door after her violently, to the amazement of the congregation. She was afterwards seen by some in their fits, who said, " O Goodwife C. I did not think to see you here!" (and being at their red bread and drink) said to her, " Is this a time to receive the Sacrament; you ran away on the Lord's-day, and scorned to receive it in the meeting-house, and is this a time to receive it? I wonder at you!" This is the sum of what I either saw myself, or did receive information from persons of undoubted reputation and credit.

Remarks of Things more than Ordinary about the Afflicted Persons.

1. They are in their fits tempted to be witches, are showed the list of the names of others, and are tortured because they will not yield to subscribe, or meddle with, or touch the book, and are promised to have present relief if they would do it.

2. They did in the assembly mutually cure each other, even with a touch of their hand, when strangled, and otherwise tortured; and would endeavour to get to their afflicted to relieve them.

3. They did also foretell when another fit was acoming, and would say, "Look to her! She will have a fit presently," which fell out accordingly, as many can bear witness that heard and saw it.

4. That at the same time when the accused person was present, the afflicted persons saw her likeness in other places of the meeting-house, sucking her familiar, sometimes in one place and posture, and sometimes in another.

5. That their motions in their fits are preternatural both as to the manner, which is so strange as a well person could not screw their body into; and as to the violence also it is preternatural, being much beyond the ordinary force of the same person when they are in their right mind.

6. The eyes of some of them in their fits are exceeding fast closed, and if you ask a question they can give no answer, and I do believe they cannot hear at that time, yet do they plainly converse with the appearances as if they did discourse with real persons.

7. They are utterly pressed against any persons

13

praying with them, and told by the appearances they
shall not go to prayer; so Thomas Putman's wife was
told, " I should not pray "; but she said, " I should ";
and after I had done, reasoned with the appearance,
" Did not I say he should go to prayer?"

8. The forementioned Mary W., being a little
better at ease, the afflicted persons said, " She had
signed the book," and that was the reason she was
better. Told me by Edward Putman.

REMARKS CONCERNING THE ACCUSED.

1. For introduction to the discovery of those that
afflicted them, it is reported Mr. Parris's Indian man
and woman made a cake of rye meal, and the children's
water, baked it in the ashes, and gave it to a dog, since
which they have discovered and seen particular persons
hurting of them.

2. In time of examination they seemed little affected,
though all the spectators were much grieved to see it.

3. Natural actions in them produced preternatural
actions in the afflicted, so that they are their own image
without any poppets of wax or otherwise.

4. That they are accused to have a company of
about twenty-three or twenty-four and they did muster
in arms, as it seemed to the afflicted persons.

5. Since they were confined the persons have not
been so much afflicted with their appearing to them,
biting or pinching of them, &c.

6. They are reported by the afflicted persons to
keep days of fast and days of thanksgiving and sacra-
ments; Satan endeavours to transform himself to an

angel of light, and to make his kingdom and adminis-
trations to resemble those of our Lord Jesus Christ.

7. Satan rages principally amongst the visible
subjects of Christ's Kingdom, and makes use (at least
in appearance) of some of them to afflict others; that
Christ's kingdom may be divided against itself, and
so be weakened.

8. Several things used in England at trial of
witches, to the number of fourteen or fifteen, which
are wont to pass instead of, or in concurrence with
witnesses, at least six or seven of them are found in
these accused: see "Keeble's Statutes."

9. Some of the most solid afflicted persons do affirm
the same things concerning seeing the accused out of
their fits, as well as in them.

10. The witches had a fast, and told one of the
afflicted girls she must not eat, because it was fast day.
She said she would; they told her they would choke
her then, which when she did eat was endeavoured.

A FURTHER ACCOUNT OF THE TRIALS OF THE NEW
ENGLAND WITCHES, SENT IN A LETTER FROM THENCE
TO A GENTLEMAN IN LONDON.

Here were in Salem, June 10, 1692, about forty
persons that were afflicted with horrible torments by
evil spirits, and the afflicted have accused sixty or
seventy as witches, for that they have spectral appearances of them, though the persons are absent when
they are tormented. When these witches were tried,
several of them confessed a contract with the devil, by
signing his book, and did express much sorrow for

the same, declaring also their confederate witches, and said the tempters of them desired them to sign the devil's book, who tormented them till they did it. There were at the time of examination, before many hundreds of witnesses, strange pranks played; such as the taking pins out of the clothes of the afflicted and thrusting them into their flesh, many of which were taken out again by the Judge's own hands. Thorns also in like kind were thrust into their flesh; the accusers were sometimes struck dumb, deaf, blind, and sometimes lay as if they were dead for a while, and all foreseen and declared by the afflicted just before it was done. Of the afflicted there were two girls, about twelve or thirteen years of age, who saw all that was done, and were therefore called the visionary girls. They would say, " Now he, or she, or they, are going to bite or pinch the Indian," and all there present in Court saw the visible marks on the Indian's arms. They would also cry out, " Now look, look, they are going to bind such an one's legs," and all present saw the same person spoken of fall with her legs twisted in an extraordinary manner. Now, say they, we shall all fall, and immediately seven or eight of the afflicted fell down, with terrible shrieks and outcries. At the time when one of the witches was sentenced and pinioned with a cord, at the same time was the afflicted Indian servant going home (being about two or three miles out of town), and had both his wrists at the same instant bound about with a like cord, in the same manner as she was when she was sentenced, but with that violence that the cord entered into his flesh, not to be untied, nor hardly cut. Many murders are supposed to be in this way committed; for these girls and others of the afflicted say they see coffins, and bodies in shrouds, rising up, and looking on the accused, crying, "Vengeance, vengeance on the murderers!" Many other strange things were transacted before the Court in the time of their examination, and especially one thing which I had like to have forgot, which is this: One of the accused, whilst the rest were under examination, was drawn up by a rope to the roof of the house where he was, and would have been choked in all probability had not the rope been presently cut; the rope hung at the roof by some invisible tie, for there was no hole where it went up; but after it was cut the remainder of it was found in the chamber just above, lying by the very place where it hung down.

In December, 1692, the Court sat again at Salem in New England, and cleared about forty persons suspected for witches, and condemned three. The evidence against these three was the same as formerly, so the warrant for their execution was sent, and the graves digged for the said three, and for about five more that had been condemned at Salem formerly, but were reprieved by the Governor.

In the beginning of February, 1693, the Court sat at Charles Town, where the Judge expressed himself to this effect: "That who it was that obstructed the execution of justice, or hindered those good proceedings they had made, he knew not, but thereby the kingdom of Satan was advanced, &c., and the Lord have mercy on this country"; and so declined coming any more into Court. In his absence Mr. D—— sat as Chief Judge three several days, in which time five or six were cleared by proclamation, and almost as many by trial; so that all are acquitted.

The most remarkable was an old woman named Dayton, of whom it was said, "If any in the world were a witch, she was one, and had been so accounted thirty years." I had the curiosity to see her tried. She was a decrepit woman of about eighty years of age, and did not use many words in her own defence. She was accused by about thirty witnesses; but the matter alleged against her was such as needed little apology. On her part, not one passionate word, or immoral action, or evil was then objected against her for twenty years past, only strange accidents falling out, after some Christian admonition given by her, as saying, "God would not prosper them if they wronged the widow." Upon the whole, there was not proved against her anything worthy of reproof, or just admonition, much less so heinous a charge.

So that by the goodness of God we are once more out of present danger of this hobgoblin monster; the standing evidence used at Salem were called, but did not appear.

There were others also at Charles Town brought upon their trials, who had formerly confessed themselves to be witches; but upon their trials denied it, and were all cleared, so that at present there is no further prosecution of any.

A Trial of Witches

AT THE ASSIZES

HELD AT

Bury St. Edmunds, for the County of Suffolk; on the
Tenth Day of March, 1664

BEFORE

Sir MATTHEW HALE, Kt.

Then Lord Chief Baron of His Majesty's Court of Exchequer

TAKEN BY A PERSON THEN ATTENDING THE COURT

TO THE READER.

This trial of witches hath lain a long time in a private gentleman's hands in the country, it being given to him by the person that took it in the Court for his own satisfaction; but it came lately to my hands, and having perused it, I found it a very remarkable thing, and fit to be published, especially in these times, wherein things of this nature are so much controverted, and that by persons of much learning on both sides. I thought that so exact a relation of this trial would probably give more satisfaction to a great many persons, by reason that it is pure matter of fact, and that evidently demonstrated, than the arguments and reasons of other very learned men, that probably may not be so intelligible to all readers; especially this being held before a Judge whom for his integrity, learning, and law hardly any age, either before or since, could parallel, who not only took a great deal of pains and spent much time in this trial himself, but had the assistance and opinion of several other very eminent and learned persons; so that this being the most perfect narrative of anything of this nature hitherto extant, made me unwilling to deprive the world of the benefit of it, which is the sole motive that induced me to publish it. Farewell.

A TRIAL OF WITCHES.

AT THE ASSIZES and General Gaol Delivery, held at
Bury St. Edmunds, for the County of Suffolk, the
Tenth of March, in the sixteenth year of the reign
of our Sovereign Lord King Charles II., before
Matthew Hale, Knight, Lord Chief Baron of His
Majesty's Court of Exchequer; Rose Cullender and
Amy Duny, widows, both of Leystoff, in the county
aforesaid, were severally indicted for bewitching
Elizabeth and Ann Durent, Jane Bocking, Susan
Chandler, William Durent, Elizabeth and Deborah
Pacy: and the said Cullender and Duny, being
arraigned upon the said indictments, pleaded
" Not guilty," and afterwards, upon a long evidence,
were found " Guilty," and thereupon had judgment
to die for the same.
The evidence whereupon these persons were convicted
of witchcraft stands upon divers particular
circumstances.

I. Three of the parties above-named, viz. Ann
Durent, Susan Chandler and Elizabeth Pacy, were
brought to Bury to the Assizes, and were in a reasonable good condition; but that morning they came into
the hall to give instructions for the drawing of their
bills of indictments, the three persons fell into strange
and violent fits, screeching out in a most sad manner,
so that they could not in any wise give any instructions

in the Court who were the cause of their distemper; and although they did after some certain space recover out of their fits, yet they were every one of them struck dumb, so that none of them could speak neither at that time, nor during the Assizes, until the conviction of the supposed witches.

As concerning William Durent, being an infant, his mother, Dorothy Durent, sworn and examined, deposed in open Court that about the tenth of March, *Nono Caroli Secundi*, she having a special occasion to go from home, and having none in her house to take care of her said child (it then sucking), desired Amy Duny, her neighbour, to look to her child during her absence, for which she promised her to give her a penny; but the said Dorothy Durent desired the same Amy not to suckle her child, and laid a great charge upon her not to do it. Upon which it was asked by the Court, Why she did give that direction, she being an old woman and not capable of giving suck? It was answered by the said Dorothy Durent that she very well knew that she did not give suck, but that for some years before she had gone under the reputation of a witch, which was one cause made her give her the caution. Another was, that it was customary with old women that if they did look after a sucking child, and nothing would please it but the breast, they did use to please the child to give it the breast; and it did please the child, but it sucked nothing but wind, which did the child hurt. Nevertheless, after the departure of this deponent, the said Amy did suckle the child; and after the return of the said Dorothy, the said Amy did acquaint her that she had given suck to the child contrary to her command. Whereupon the deponent was very angry with the said

Amy for the same; at which the said Amy was much
discontented, and used many high expressions and
threatening speeches towards her, telling her that she
had as good to have done otherwise than to have found
fault with her, and so departed out of her house. And
that very night her son fell into strange fits of swooning,
and was held in such terrible manner that she was much
affrighted therewith, and so continued for divers weeks.
And the said examinant further said, that she being
exceedingly troubled at her child's distemper, did go
to a certain person named Doctor Jacob, who lived at
Yarmouth, who had the reputation in the country to
help children that were bewitched, who advised her
to hang up the child's blanket in the chimney corner
all day, and at night, when she put the child to bed,
to put it into the said blanket, and if she found anything
in it she should not be afraid, but to throw it into the
fire. And this deponent did according to his direction;
and at night, when she took down the blanket with an
intent to put her child therein, there fell out of the
same a great toad, which ran up and down the hearth,
and she, having a young youth only with her in the
house, desired him to catch the toad and throw it into
the fire, which the youth did accordingly, and held it
there with the tongs; and as soon as it was in the fire
it made a great and horrible noise, and after a space
there was a flashing in the fire like gunpowder, making
a noise like the discharge of a pistol, and thereupon
the toad was no more seen nor heard. It was asked
by the Court if that after the noise and flashing there
was not the substance of the toad to be seen to con-
sume in the fire? And it was answered by the said
Dorothy Durent, that after the flashing and noise there
was no more seen than if there had been none there.

The next day there came a young woman, a kinswoman of the said Amy and a neighbour of this deponent, and told this deponent that her aunt (meaning the said Amy) was in a most lamentable condition, having her face all scorched with fire, and that she was sitting alone in her house in her smock without any fire. And thereupon this deponent went into the house of the said Amy Duny to see her, and found her in the same condition as was related to her, for her face, her legs, and thighs, which this deponent saw, seemed very much scorched and burnt with fire, at which this deponent seemed much to wonder, and asked the said Amy how she came into that sad condition; and the said Amy replied she might thank her for it, for that she, this deponent, was the cause thereof, but that she should live to see some of her children dead and she upon crutches. And this deponent further saith that after the burning of the said toad her child recovered, and was well again, and was living at the time of the Assizes. And this deponent further saith that about the 6th of March, 11 Car. 2, her daughter, Elizabeth Durent, being about the age of ten years, was taken in like manner as her first child was, and in her fits complained much of Amy Duny, and said that she did appear to her and afflict her in such manner as the former; and she, this deponent, going to the apothecaries for something for her said child, when she did return to her own house she found the said Amy Duny there, and asked her what she did do there, and her answer was, that she came to see her child, and to give it some water. But she, this deponent, was very angry with her, and thrust her forth of her doors; and when she was out of doors she said, "You need not be so angry, for your child will not live long." And this was on a Saturday, and the child died on the Monday following, the cause of whose death this deponent verily believeth was occasioned by the witchcraft of the said Amy Duny, for that the said Amy hath been long reputed to be a witch and a person of very evil behaviour, whose kindred and relations have been many of them accused for witchcraft, and some of them have been condemned.

The said deponent further saith that not long after the death of her daughter, Elizabeth Durent, she, this deponent, was taken with a lameness in both her legs from the knees downward; that she was fain to go upon crutches; and that she had no other use of them but only to bear a little upon them till she did remove her crutches, and so continued till the time of the Assizes that the witch came to be tried, and was there upon her crutches. The Court asked her, " That at the time she was taken with this lameness, if it were with her according to the custom of women?" Her answer was that it was so, and that she never had any stoppages of those things but when she was with child.

This is the substance of her evidence to this indictment.

There was one thing very remarkable—that after she had gone upon crutches for upwards of three years, and went upon them at the time of the Assizes in the Court, when she gave her evidence, and upon the jury's bringing in their verdict, by which the said Amy Duny was found guilty, to the great admiration of all persons the said Dorothy Durent was restored to the use of her limbs, and went home without making use of her crutches.

II. As concerning Elizabeth and Deborah Pacy, the first of the age of eleven years, the other of the

age of nine years or thereabouts, as to the elder, she
was brought into the Court at the time of the instructions given to draw up the indictments and afterwards
at the time of trial of the said prisoners, but could not
speak one word all the time, and, for the most part,
she remained as one wholly senseless, as one in a deep
sleep, and could move no part of her body, and all the
motion of life that appeared in her was, that as she
lay upon cushions in the Court upon her back her
stomach and belly, by the drawing of her breath, would
arise to a great height; and after the said Elizabeth
had lain a long time on the table in the Court she came
a little to herself and sat up, but could neither see nor
speak, but was sensible of what was said to her; and
after a while she laid her head on the bar of the Court
with a cushion under it, and her hand and her apron
upon that, and there she lay a good space of time.
And by the direction of the Judge, Amy Duny was
privately brought to Elizabeth Pacy, and she touched
her hand; whereupon the child, without so much as
seeing her, for her eyes were closed all the while,
suddenly leaped up and catched Amy Duny by the
hand, and afterwards by the face, and with her nails
scratched her till blood came, and would by no means
leave her till she was taken from her; and afterwards
the child would still be pressing towards her, and
making signs of anger conceived against her.

Deborah the younger daughter was held in such
extreme manner that her parents wholly despaired
of her life, and therefore could not bring her to the
Assizes.

The evidence which was given concerning these
two children was to this effect:

Samuel Pacy, a merchant of Leystoff aforesaid (a
man who carried himself with much soberness during
the trial, from whom proceeded no words either of
passion or malice, though his children were so greatly
afflicted), sworn and examined, deposed that his
younger daughter Deborah, upon Thursday, the tenth
of October last, was suddenly taken with a lameness
in her legs, so that she could not stand, neither had
she any strength in her limbs to support her; and so
she continued until the seventeenth day of the same
month, which day, being fair and sunshiny, the child
desired to be carried on the east part of the house,
to be set upon the bank which looketh upon the sea;
and whilst she was sitting there Amy Duny came to
this deponent's house to buy some herrings, but being
denied she went away discontented, and presently
returned again, and was denied, and likewise the third
time, and was denied as at first; and at her last going
away she went away grumbling, but what she said was
not perfectly understood. But at the very same instant
of time the said child was taken with most violent fits,
feeling most extreme pain in her stomach, like the
pricking of pins, and shrieking out in a most dreadful
manner like unto a whelp, and not like unto a sensible
creature. And in this extremity the child continued,
to the great grief of the parents, until the thirtieth of
the same month. During this time this deponent sent
for one Dr. Feavor, a doctor of physic, to take his
advice concerning his child's distemper; the doctor,
being come, he saw the child in those fits, but could
not conjecture (as he then told this deponent, and
afterwards affirmed in open Court at this trial) what
might be the cause of the child's affliction. And this
deponent further said, that by reason of the circum-

14

stances aforesaid, and in regard Amy Duny is a woman of an ill fame and commonly reported to be a witch and sorceress, and for that the said child in her fits would cry out of Amy Duny as the cause of her malady, and that she did affright her with apparitions of her person (as the child in the intervals of her fits related), he, this deponent, did suspect the said Amy Duny for a witch, and charged her with the injury and wrong to his child, and caused her to be set in the stocks on the twenty-eighth day of the same October. And during the time of her continuance there, one Alice Letteridge and Jane Buxton, demanding of her (as they also affirmed in Court upon their oaths) what should be the reason of Mr. Pacy's child's distemper, telling her that she was suspected to be the cause thereof, she replied, " Mr. Pacy keeps a great stir about his child, but let him stay until he hath done as much by his children as I have done by mine." And being further examined what she had done to her children, she answered, " That she had been fain to open her child's mouth with a tap to give it victuals."

And the said deponent further deposeth that within two days after speaking of the said words, being the thirtieth of October, the eldest daughter, Elizabeth, fell into extreme fits, insomuch that they could not open her mouth to give her breath to preserve her life without the help of a tap, which they were enforced to use; and the younger child was in the like manner afflicted, so that they used the same also for her relief.

And, further, the said children, being grievously afflicted, would severally complain in their extremity, and also in the intervals, that Amy Duny (together with one other woman, whose person and clothes they described) did thus afflict them, their apparitions appearing before them, to their great terror and affrightment; and sometimes they would cry out, saying, "There stands Amy Duny, and there Rose Cullender," the other person troubling them.

Their fits were various. Sometimes they would be lame on one side of their bodies, sometimes on the other; sometimes a soreness over their whole bodies, so as they could endure none to touch them. At other times they would be restored to the perfect use of their limbs, and deprived of their hearing; at other times of their sight; at other times of their speech, sometimes by the space of one day, sometimes for two; and once they were wholly deprived of their speech for eight days together, and then restored to their speech again. At other times they would fall into swoonings, and upon the recovery to their speech they would cough extremely and bring up much phlegm, and with the same crooked pins, and one time a twopenny nail with a very broad head, which pins (amounting to forty or more), together with the twopenny nail, were produced in Court, with the affirmation of the said deponent, that he was present when the said nail was vomited up, and also most of the pins. Commonly at the end of every fit they would cast up a pin, and sometimes they would have four or five fits in one day.

In this manner the said children continued with this deponent for the space of two months, during which time, in their intervals, this deponent would cause them to read some chapters in the New Testament. Whereupon this deponent several times observed that they would read till they came to the name of Lord, or Jesus, or Christ, and then before they could pronounce either of the said words they would suddenly fall into their fits. But when they

came to the name of Satan, or Devil, they would clap
their fingers upon the book, crying out, "This bites,
but makes me speak right well."

At such time as they be recovered out of their fits
(occasioned, as this deponent conceives, upon their
naming of Lord, or Jesus, or Christ), this deponent
hath demanded of them, what is the cause they cannot
pronounce these words? They reply and say, "That
Amy Duny saith, I must not use that name."

And, further, the said children, after their fits were
past, would tell how that Amy Duny and Rose
Cullender would appear before them, holding their
fists at them, threatening, "That if they related either
what they saw or heard, they would torment them
ten times more than ever they did before."

In their fits they would cry out, "There stands
Amy Duny or Rose Cullender," and sometimes in one
place and sometimes in another, running with great
violence to the place where they fancied them to stand,
striking at them as if they were present; they would
appear to them sometimes spinning, and sometimes
reeling, or in other postures, deriding or threatening
them.

And this deponent further said, that his children,
being thus tormented by all the space aforesaid, and
finding no hopes of amendment, he sent them to his
sister's house, one Margaret Arnold, who lived at
Yarmouth, to make trial whether the change of the
air might do them any good, and how, and in what
manner they were afterwards held, he, this deponent,
refers himself to the testimony of his said sister.

Margaret Arnold, sworn and examined, said that
the said Elizabeth and Deborah Pacy came to her
house about the thirtieth of November last. Her

brother acquainted her that he thought they were
bewitched, for that they vomited pins, and further
informed her of the several passages which occurred
at his own house.   This deponent said that she gave
no credit to that which was related to her, conceiving
possibly the children might use some deceit in putting
pins in their mouths themselves.   Wherefore this
deponent unpinned all their clothes, and left not so
much as one pin upon them, but sewed all the clothes
they wore, instead of pinning of them.   But this
deponent said that, notwithstanding all this care and
circumspection of hers, the children afterwards raised
at several times at least thirty pins in her presence,
and had most fierce and violent fits upon them.

The children would in their fits cry out against
Rose Cullender and Amy Duny, affirming that they
saw them, and they threatened to torment them ten
times more if they complained of them.   At some times
the children (only) would see things run up and down
the house in the appearance of mice, and one of them
suddenly snapped one with the tongs and threw it into
the fire, and it screeched out like a rat.

At another time the younger child, being out of
her fits, went out of doors to take a little fresh air,
and presently a little thing like a bee flew upon her
face, and would have gone into her mouth, whereupon
the child ran in all haste to the door to get into the
house again, screeching out in a most terrible manner.
Whereupon this deponent made haste to come to her,
but before she could get to her the child fell into her
swooning fit, and at last, with much pain straining
herself, she vomited up a twopenny nail with a broad
head; and after that the child had raised up the nail
she came to her understanding, and being demanded

by this deponent how she came by this nail, she answered, "That the bee brought this nail and forced it into her mouth."

And ,at other times the elder child declared unto this deponent that during the time of her fits she saw flies come unto her, and bring with them in their mouths crooked pins; and after the child had thus declared the same she fell again into violent fits, and afterwards raised several pins.

At another time the said elder child declared unto this deponent, and sitting by the fire suddenly started up and said she saw a mouse, and she crept under the table looking after it, and at length she put something in her apron, saying she had caught it; and immediately she ran to the fire and threw it in, and there did appear upon it to this deponent like the flashing of gunpowder, though she confessed she saw nothing in the child's hand.

At another time the said child, being speechless, but otherwise of perfect understanding, ran round about the house holding her apron, crying, "Hush, hush," as if there had been some poultry in the house, but this deponent could perceive nothing. But at last she saw the child stoop, as if she had caught at something, and put it into her apron, and afterwards made as if she had thrown it into the fire. But this deponent could not discover anything; but the child afterwards being restored to her speech, she, this deponent, demanded of her what she saw at the time she used such a posture, who answered, "That she saw a duck."

At another time the younger daughter, being recovered out of her fits, declared that Amy Duny had been with her, and that she tempted her to drown herself, and to cut her throat, or otherwise to destroy herself.

At another time in their fits they both of them cried out upon Rose Cullender and Amy Duny, complaining against them, "Why do not you come yourselves, but send your imps to torment us?"

These several passages, as most remarkable, the said deponent did particularly set down as they daily happened, and for the reasons aforesaid she doth verily believe in her conscience that the children were bewitched, and by the said Amy Duny and Rose Cullender, though at first she could hardly be induced to believe it.

As concerning Ann Durent, one other of the parties, supposed to be bewitched, present in Court:

Edmund Durent, her father, sworn and examined, said that he also lived in the said town of Leystoff, and that the said Rose Cullender, about the latter end of November last, came into this deponent's house to buy some herrings of his wife, but being denied by her, the said Rose returned in a discontented manner; and upon the first of December after his daughter, Ann Durent, was very sorely afflicted in her stomach, and felt great pain like the pricking of pins, and then fell into swooning fits, and after the recovery from her fits she declared that she had seen the apparition of the said Rose, who threatened to torment her. In this manner she continued from the first of December until this present time of trial, having likewise vomited up divers pins (produced here in Court). This maid was present in Court, but could not speak to declare her knowledge, but fell into most violent fits when she was brought before Rose Cullender.

Ann Baldwin, sworn and examined, deposed the same thing as touching the bewitching of the said Ann Durent.

As concerning Jane Bocking, who was so weak she could not be brought to the Assizes:

Diana Bocking, sworn and examined, deposed that she lived in the same town of Leystoff, and that her said daughter, having been formerly afflicted with swooning fits, recovered well of them, and so continued for a certain time; and upon the first of February last she was taken also with great pain in her stomach, like pricking with pins, and afterwards fell into swooning fits, and so continued till the deponent's coming to the Assizes, having during the same time taken little or no food, but daily vomited crooked pins, and upon Sunday last raised seven pins. And whilst her fits were upon her she would spread forth her arms with her hands open, and used postures as if she catched at something, and instantly closed her hands again, which, being immediately forced open, they found several pins diversely crooked, but could neither see nor perceive how or in what manner they were conveyed thither. At another time the same Jane, being in another of her fits, talked as if she were discoursing with some persons in the room (though she would give no answer nor seem to take notice of any person then present), and would in like manner cast abroad her arms, saying, "I will not have it; I will not have it"; and at last she said, "Then I will have it." And so, waving her arm with her hand open, she would presently close the same, which, instantly forced open, they found in it a lath nail. In her fits she would frequently complain of Rose Cullender and Amy Duny, saying that now she saw Rose Cullender standing at the bed's foot, and another time at the bed's head, and so in other places. At last she was stricken dumb and could not speak one word, though her fits were not upon her, and so she continued for some days; and at last her speech came to her again, and she desired her mother to get her some meat; and being demanded the reason why she could not speak in so long time, she answered, "That Amy Duny would not suffer her to speak." This lath nail and divers of the pins were produced in Court.

As concerning Susan Chandler, one other of the parties supposed to be bewitched and present in Court:

Mary Chandler, mother of the said Susan, sworn and examined, deposed and said that about the beginning of February last past the said Rose Cullender and Amy Duny were charged by Mr. Samuel Pacy for bewitching of his daughters, and a warrant being granted at the request of the said Mr. Pacy by Sir Edmund Bacon, Bart., one of the Justices of the peace for the county of Suffolk, to bring them before him; they, being brought before him, were examined, and confessed nothing. He gave order that they should be searched; whereupon this deponent, with five others, were appointed to do the same. And coming to the house of Rose Cullender, they did acquaint her with what they were come about, and asked whether she was contented that they should search her. She did not oppose it; whereupon they began at her head, and so stripped her naked, and in the lower part of her belly they found a thing like a teat of an inch long. They questioned her about it, and she said that she had got a strain by carrying of water, which caused that excrescence. But upon narrower search they found in her privy parts three more excrescences or teats, but smaller than the former. This deponent further said that in the long teat, at the end thereof, there was a little hole, and it appeared unto them as if it had been lately sucked, and upon the straining of it there issued out white milky matter.

And this deponent further saith that her said daughter (being of the age of eighteen years) was then in service in the said town of Leystoff, and rising up early the next morning to wash, this Rose Cullender appeared to her and took her by the hand, whereat she was much affrighted, and went forthwith to her mother (being in the same town) and acquainted her with what she had seen; but being extremely terrified she fell extremely sick, much grieved at her stomach; and that night, after being in bed with another young woman, she suddenly shrieked out and fell into such extreme fits as if she were distracted, crying against Rose Cullender, saying she would come to bed to her. She continued in this manner, beating and wearing herself, insomuch that this deponent was glad to get help to attend her. In her intervals she would declare that some time she saw Rose Cullender, at another time with a great dog with her. She also vomited up divers crooked pins; and sometimes she was stricken with blindness, and at another time she was dumb, and so she appeared to be in Court when the trial of the prisoners was, for she was not able to speak her knowledge; but being brought into the Court at the trial, she suddenly fell into her fits, and being carried out of the Court again within the space of half an hour she came to herself and recovered her speech, and thereupon was immediately brought into the Court, and asked by the Court whether she was in condition to take an oath and to give evidence; she said she could. But when she was sworn and asked what she could say against either of the prisoners, before she could make any answer she fell into her fits, shrieking out in a miserable manner, crying, "Burn her, burn her," which were all the words she could speak.

Robert Chandler, father of the said Susan, gave in the same evidence that his wife, Mary Chandler, had given, only as to the searching of Rose Cullender as aforesaid.

This was the sum and substance of the evidence which was given against the prisoners concerning the bewitching of the children before-mentioned. At the hearing this evidence there were divers known persons, as Mr. Serjeant Keeling, Mr. Serjeant Earl, and Mr. Serjeant Barnard, present. Mr. Serjeant Keeling seemed much unsatisfied with it, and thought it not sufficient to convict the prisoners. For, admitting that the children were in truth bewitched, yet, said he, it can never be applied to the prisoners upon the imagination only of the parties afflicted. For if that might be allowed, no person whatsoever can be in safety, for perhaps they might fancy another person, who might altogether be innocent in such matters.

There was also Dr. Brown, of Norwich, a person of great knowledge, who, after this evidence given and upon view of the three persons in Court, was desired to give his opinion what he did conceive of them. And he was clearly of opinion that the persons were bewitched, and said that in Denmark there had been lately a great discovery of witches, who used the very same way of afflicting persons by conveying pins into them, and crooked as these pins were, with needles and nails. And his opinion was that the devil in such cases did work upon the bodies of men and women upon a natural foundation; that is, to stir up and excite such humours superabounding in their bodies to a great excess, whereby he did in an extraordinary manner afflict them with such distempers as their bodies were most subject to, as particularly appeared in these children; for he conceived that these swooning fits were natural, and nothing else but that they call the mother, but only heightened to a great excess by the subtilty of the devil, co-operating with the malice of these which we term witches, at whose instance he doth these villainies.

Besides the particulars above-mentioned touching the said persons bewitched, there were many other things objected against them for a further proof and manifestation that the said children were bewitched.

At first, during the time of the trial, there were some experiments made with the persons afflicted by bringing the persons to touch them; and it was observed that when they were in the midst of their fits, to all men's apprehension wholly deprived of all sense and understanding, closing their fists in such manner as that the strongest man in the Court could not force them open, yet by the least touch of one of those supposed witches, Rose Cullender by name, they would suddenly shriek out, opening their hands, which accident would not happen by the touch of any other person.

And lest they might privately see when they were touched by the said Rose Cullender they were blinded with their own aprons, and the touching took the same effect as before.

There was an ingenious person that objected.
There might be a great fallacy in this experiment,
and there ought not to be any stress put upon this to
convict the parties, for the children might counterfeit
this their distemper, and perceiving what was done
to them they might in such manner suddenly alter the
motion and gesture of their bodies on purpose to
induce persons to believe that they were not natural,
but wrought strangely by the touch of the prisoners.

Wherefore to avoid this scruple it was privately
desired by the Judge that the Lord Cornwallis,
Sir Edmund Bacon, and Mr. Serjeant Keeling, and
some other gentlemen there in Court, would attend
one of the distempered persons in the farther part of
the hall whilst she was in her fits, and then to send
for one of the witches to try what would then happen,
which they did accordingly; and Amy Duny was conveyed from the bar and brought to the maid.   They
put an apron before her eyes, and then one other
person touched her hand, which produced the same
effect as the touch of the witch did in the Court.
Whereupon the gentlemen returned, openly protesting
that they did believe the whole transaction of this
business was a mere imposture.

This put the Court and all persons into a stand.
But at length Mr. Pacy did declare that possibly the
maid might be deceived by a suspicion that the witch
touched her when she did not.   For he had observed
divers times that although they could not speak, but
were deprived of the use of their tongues and limbs,
that their understandings were perfect, for that they
have related divers things which have been when they
were in their fits after they were recovered out of them.
This saying of Mr. Pacy was found to be true after-

wards, when his daughter was fully recovered (as she afterwards was), as shall in due time be related. For she was asked whether she did hear or understand anything that was done and acted in the Court during the time that she lay as one deprived of her understanding, and she said she did. And by the opinions of some this experiment (which others would have a fallacy) was rather a confirmation that the parties were really bewitched than otherwise, for, say they, it is not possible that any should counterfeit such distempers, being accompanied with such various circumstances, much less children, and for so long time, and yet undiscovered by their parents and relations; for no man can suppose that they should all conspire together (being out of several families, and, as they affirm, no way related one to the other, and scarce of familiar acquaintance) to do an act of this nature, whereby no benefit or advantage could redound to any of the parties, but a guilty conscience for perjuring themselves in taking the lives of two poor simple women away; and there appears no malice in the case, for the prisoners themselves did scarce so much as object it. Wherefore, say they, it is very evident that the parties were bewitched, and that when they apprehend or understand by any means that the persons who have done them this wrong are near, or touch them, then their spirits, being more than ordinarily moved with rage and anger at them being present, they do use more violent gestures of their bodies, and extend forth their hands as desirous to lay hold upon them, which at other times, not having the same occasion, the instance there falls not out the same.

Secondly, one John Soam, of Leystoff aforesaid, yeoman, a sufficient person, deposed that not long since, in harvest time, he had three carts, which brought home his harvest; and as they were going into the field to load one of the carts wrenched the window of Rose Cullender's house, whereupon she came out in a great rage and threatened this deponent for doing that wrong; and so they passed along into the fields and loaded all the three carts. The other two carts returned safe home and back again, twice loaded that day afterwards; but as to this cart which touched Rose Cullender's house, after it was loaded it was overturned twice or thrice that day; and after that they had loaded it again the second or third time, as they brought it through the gate which leads out of the field into the town, the cart stuck so fast in the gate's head that they could not possibly get it through, but were enforced to cut down the post of the gate to make the cart pass through, although they could not perceive that the cart did of either side touch the gate posts. And this deponent further said that after they had got it through the gateway they did with much difficulty get it home into the yard; but for all that they could do they could not get the cart near unto the place where they should unload the corn, but were fain to unload it at a great distance from the place, and when they began to unload they found much difficulty therein, it being so hard a labour that they were tired that first came, and when others came to assist them their noses burst forth a-bleeding. So they were fain to desist and leave it until the next morning, and then they unloaded it without any difficulty at all.

Robert Sherringham also deposed against Rose Cullender that about two years since, passing along the street with his cart and horses, the axle-tree of his cart touched her house and broke down some part of it, at which she was very much displeased, threatening him that his horses should suffer for it; and so it happened, for all those horses, being four in number, died within a short time after. Since that time he had had great losses by the sudden dying of his other cattle; so soon as his sows pigged the pigs would leap and caper, and immediately fall down and die. Also, not long after, he was taken with a lameness in his limbs that he could neither go nor stand for some days. After all this he was very much vexed with great number of lice of an extraordinary bigness, and although he many times shifted himself, yet he was not anything the better, but would swarm again with them, so that in the conclusion he was forced to burn all his clothes, being two suits of apparel, and then was clean from them.

As concerning Amy Duny, one Richard Spencer deposed that about the first of September last he heard her say at his house that the devil would not let her rest until she were revenged on one Cornelius Sandeswell's wife.

Ann Sandeswell, wife unto the abovesaid Cornelius, deposed that about seven or eight years since, she having bought a certain number of geese, meeting with Amy Duny, she told her if she did not fetch her geese home they would all be destroyed, which in a few days after came to pass.

Afterwards the said Amy became tenant to this deponent's husband for a house, who told her that if she looked not well to such a chimney in her house that the same would fall. Whereupon this deponent replied that it was a new one; but not minding much her words, at that time they parted. But in a short time the chimney fell down, according as the said Amy had said.

Also this deponent further said that her brother, being a fisherman, and using to go into the northern seas, she desired him to send her a firkin of fish, which he did accordingly; and she having notice that the said firkin was brought into Leystoff Road, she desired a boatman to bring it ashore with the other goods they were to bring; and she, going down to meet the boatman to receive her fish, desired the said Amy to go along with her to help her home with it. Amy replied, "She would go when she had it"; and thereupon this deponent went to the shore without her, and demanded of the boatman the firkin. They told her that they could not keep it in the boat from falling into the sea, and they thought it was gone to the devil, for they never saw the like before. And being demanded by this deponent whether any goods in the boat were likewise lost as well as hers, they answered, "Not any."

This was the substance of the whole evidence given against the prisoners at the bar, who, being demanded what they had to say for themselves, they replied, "Nothing material to anything that was proved against them." Whereupon the Judge, in giving his direction to the jury, told them that he would not repeat the evidence unto them, lest by so doing he should wrong the evidence on the one side or on the other. Only this acquainted them that they had two things to enquire after: First, whether or no these children were bewitched? Secondly, whether the prisoners at the bar were guilty of it?

15

That there were such creatures as witches he made no doubt at all, for, first, the Scriptures had affirmed so much. Secondly, the wisdom of all nations had provided laws against such persons, which is an argument of their confidence of such a crime. And such has been the judgment of this kingdom, as appears by that Act of Parliament, which has proved punishments proportionable to the quality of the offence, and desired them strictly to observe their evidence, and desired the great God of Heaven to direct their hearts in this weighty thing they had in hand: "For to condemn the innocent, and to let the guilty go free, were both an abomination to the Lord."

With this short direction the jury departed from the bar, and within the space of half an hour returned, and brought them in both "Guilty" upon the several indictments, which were thirteen in number, where-upon they stood indicted.

This was upon Thursday, in the afternoon, March 13, 1662.

The next morning the three children, with their parents, came to the Lord Chief Baron Hale's lodging, who all of them spake perfectly, and were in as good health as ever they were; only Susan Chandler, by reason of her very much affliction, did look very thin and wan. And their friends were asked at what time they were restored thus to their speech and health, and Mr. Pacy did affirm, that within less than half an hour after the witches were convicted they were all of them restored, and slept well that night, feeling no pain. Only Susan Chandler felt a pain like pricking of pins in her stomach.

After, they were all of them brought down to the Court, but Ann Durent was so fearful to behold them that she desired she might not see them. The other two continued in the Court, and they affirmed in the face of the country, and before the witches themselves, what before had been deposed by their friends and relations, the prisoners not much contradicting them. In conclusion, the Judge and all the Court were fully satisfied with the verdict, and thereupon gave judgment against the witches that they should be hanged.

They were much urged to confess, but would not.

That morning we departed for Cambridge, but no reprieve was granted; and they were executed on Monday, the seventeenth of March following, but they confessed nothing.

PART III.

AMUSING ACTIONS AT LAW.

Sir Thomas Holt *versus* Astrigg.

Michaelmas Term, 1607.

Action upon the case for words: " Sir Thomas Holt struck his cook on the head with a cleaver, and cleaved his head; the one part lay on the one shoulder, and another part on the other." The defendant pleaded " Not guilty," and found against him; and now moved in arrest of judgment that these words were not actionable, for it is not averred that the cook was killed, but argumentative; and of that opinion was the Court, for slander ought to be direct, against which there may not be any intendment. But here, notwithstanding such wounding, the party may yet be living, and it is then but trespass; wherefore it was adjudged for the defendant.

Selby *versus* Carrier.

Easter Term, 1614.

Action for these words: " Thou art a bankrupt knave." Upon " Not guilty " pleaded and found for the plaintiff, and a motion in arrest of judgment that the words were not actionable, it was held by the

Court that the words were scandalous and actionable,
being two substantives. Otherwise it had been, if the
words had been "bankruptly knave," or had been
adjectively spoken, and judgment was given for the
plaintiff.

FOSTER *versus* BROWNING.

Trinity Term, 1624.

Action for these words: "Thou art as arrant a
thief as any is in England, for thou hast broken up
I. S. Chest, and taken away 40*l*." After verdict it
was moved in arrest of judgment, because he doth not
aver that there was any thief in England; and the last
words do not import any felony, for he sheweth not
that he stole any money or robbed him of any money;
and therefore all the Justices held that the action lay
not, for it is not to be maintained by intendment, but
by express words, for the first words without an
averment will not maintain an action. And the words
do not prove any felony to be committed, for the
money may be taken away and the chest broken
open upon pretence of title, and in the midday, and
presence of divers, and then it is not any felony.
Therefore Hobert, Chief Justice, put the case: "If one
saith, 'Thou art a thief, for thou hast taken away
my corn,' action lies not, for the taking away may be
lawful. But if he had said, 'For thou hast stolen
my corn,' action lies, for it shall be intended corn
thrashed, and not in the sheafs." Wherefore it was
adjudged for the defendant.

ROBINS *versus* HILDREDON.

Easter Term, 1605.

Action for words : " Thou art a thievish knave, and
hast stolen my wood." After verdict for the plaintiff
upon " Not guilty " pleaded, and twenty marks
damages, it was moved that the action lay not, for the
words " thievish knave " will not bear an action, for it is
but an adjective to " knave "; and these words, " Thou
hast stolen my wood," are not actionable, for stealing
of wood may be intended growing wood, and then it
is not any felony, and so no cause of action.

But it was afterwards moved again for the plaintiffs that the action was well brought, for the words
" Thou hast stolen my wood " shall be intended and
be taken *in malam partem*—that he stole wood felled
—for it is not wood as long as it is growing. Also
by the statute, if one steals wood which is growing,
he is to be punished by whipping, for which cause it
is a great slander; and therefore, &c. And of that
opinion were Fenner and Yelverton, but Popham,
Gawdy, and Williams *è contra*, that the action lies
not, for although it be said that he is a thief, it being
coupled with the words subsequent, which expound
it to be no felony, those words will not maintain an
action. But if he had said that he was a thief
generally, without more, it would have been actionable, and the words, " And thou hast stolen my wood,"
is all one, as if he had said, " For thou hast stolen
my wood," which is not felony, unless it be shewn to
be wood felled, no more than if he had said, " Thou
hast stolen my apples," which are intended growing,
&c., which cannot be felony and then not actionable.

Wherefore, for the opinion of the three said Justices, it was adjudged for the defendant, *postea.*

WOLVERSTON *versus* MERES.

Hilary Term, 1601.

Action for words: "Edmond Wolverston is a bankrupt knave." It was adjudged that the action lay, he shewing that he was a merchant; and it was affirmed on a writ of error, although it was alleged that he did not say he was a bankrupt, but a bankrupt knave, which is an adjective, and it may be a bankrupt in knavery.

WATS *versus* BRAINS.

Michaelmas Term, 1600.

Appeal of murder for the death of her husband. The defendant pleaded "Not guilty," and upon evidence at the bar it appeared that two days before her husband's death he and the defendant, fighting upon a quarrel then betwixt them, the defendant was hurt in that fray; and the third day after the plaintiff's husband, passing by the defendant's shop, the defendant pursued him suddenly, and the husband's back being towards him, so as he perceived him not, the defendant struck him upon the calf of his leg, whereof he instantly died. The defendant, to excuse himself, affirmed that he who was slain, when he came by his shop, smiled upon him and wryed his mouth at him, and therefore for this mocking of him he pursued him.

And it was much enforced by the defendant's counsel that it was a new cause of quarrel; and so the stroke is not upon any precedent malice, and therefore it is not murder. But all the Court severally delivered their opinions, that if one make a wry or distorted mouth or the like countenance upon another, and the other immediately pursues and kills him, it is murder, for it shall be presumed to be malice precedent; and that such a slight provocation was not sufficient ground or pretence for a quarrel, and so delivered the law to the jury that it was murder, although what the defendant pretended had been true.

Whereupon the jury going from the bar, notwithstanding the evidence was pregnant against the defendant, eight of them agreed to find him " Not guilty "; but the other four withstood them, and would not find it but to be murder. And on the next-day morning two of the four agreed with the eight to find him " Not guilty." And afterwards the other two consented in this manner, that they should bring in and offer their verdict " Not guilty," and if the Court disliked thereof, that then they all should change the verdict and find him " Guilty "; and upon this agreement they came to the bar, and the foreman pronounced the verdict that the defendant was " Not guilty." And the Court, much misliking thereof, being contrary to their direction, examined every one of them by the poll whether that was his verdict; and ten of the first part of the panel severally affirmed their verdict, that the defendant was " Not guilty," but the two last affirmed how they agreed and discovered the whole manner of their agreement. Whereupon they were sent back again, and returned and found the defendant " Guilty."

And for this practice Harris, the foreman, was afterwards fined 100 mark, and the other seven who agreed with him at the first, every of them was fined 40*l.*; and the other two who agreed with the eight, although they affirmed that it was because they could not endure or hold out any longer, yet for that they did not discover the practice, being examined by poll, but affirmed the verdict, were fined each of them at 20*l.*, and all of them imprisoned. But the other two were dismissed, yet blamed for such a manner of consenting in abuse of the Court. And afterwards the defendant was adjudged to be hanged.

THE EASTERN PRESS, LIMITED, LONDON AND READING.

www.ingramcontent.com/pod-product-compliance
Lightning Source LLC
Chambersburg PA
CBHW030530100426
42813CB00001B/202